Crisp Toasts

D1624378

**Also by William R. Evans III
and Andrew Frothingham**

Well-Done Roasts
And I Quote (with Ashton Applewhite)

Crisp Toasts

**Wonderful Words That Add Wit and Class
Every Time You Raise Your Glass**

By William R. Evans III
Andrew Frothingham

WEST BEND LIBRARY

St. Martin's Press
New York

CRISP TOASTS. Copyright © 1992 by William R. Evans III and Andrew Frothingham. All rights reserved. Printed in the United States of America. No part of this book may be used or reproduced in any manner whatsoever without written permission except in the case of brief quotations embodied in critical articles or reviews. For information, address St. Martin's Press, 175 Fifth Avenue, New York, N.Y. 10010.

Production Editor: David Stanford Burr

Library of Congress Cataloging-in-Publication Data

Evans, William R,

Frothingham, Andrew.

    Crisp toasts : wonderful words that add wit and class to every
time you raise your glass / Andrew Frothingham and William R. Evans
III.

        p. cm.
    "A Thomas Dunne Book."
    ISBN 0-312-08171-5
    1. Toasts. I. Evans, Tripp. II. Title.
PN6341.F76 1992   I. Frothingham, Andrew.
808.5'1—dc20   92-26159
                                                          CIP

First edition: November 1992

10 9 8 7 6 5 4 3 2 1

808. 51
Ev1

We raise a glass
to those who raised us.

CONTENTS

vii

SYNONYM TOAST

INTRODUCTION

Here's to toasts! They're the words that turn the act of drinking into festive occasions and treasured memories. They're a germ-free way to share a drink and a superb way to make a friendly social statement. No matter what you want to say, you'll find just the right words in *Crisp Toasts*.

Toasts can be funny or serious. All good toasts, however, have one thing in common: they're short. A toast is not a speech. Don't ramble on. Your toast's effectiveness decreases as your audience waits—arms outstretched, glasses raised—for you to deliver it.

The toasts in this book cover the gamut from the righteous ("To eat, to drink, and be merry."—Ecclesiastes 8:15) to the risqué ("Here's to hell!/May the stay there/Be as much fun as the way there!"), from the classic ("'Twas ever thus from childhood's hour,/I've seen my fond hopes disappear;/I've always had a champagne thirst,/But have to be content with beer") to the contemporary ("In the words of *Star Trek*'s Mr. Spock, 'Live long and prosper'"). You'll have no trouble finding a toast that's appropriate to the audience and the event.

HOW THIS BOOK IS ORGANIZED

The book is divided into occasion-specific categories. In the front of the book there are two reference lists. The first, the CONTENTS, presents the categories as they appear in the book. If you can't find your topic there, look it up in the second list, SYNONYM TOAST (get it?). This list will direct you to the appropriate category in the book. For instance, "company" does not appear in the CONTENTS, so turn to SYNONYM TOAST, find "company" and you'll be directed to "GUESTS." You'll notice that all categories in the book are in upper case, while synonyms are in lower case.

Some of the material appears in more than one section. We did this on purpose so you wouldn't waste time rummaging through the book chasing cross-references.

The toasts in this book are in three basic forms. One form incorporates a quote and an attribution in the toast (for example, "To action. As Benjamin Disraeli said, 'Action may not always bring happiness, but there is no happiness without action'"). In cases where a quote is strong enough or sufficiently familiar to stand alone, the author is identified following the quote (for example, "A book of verses underneath the bough,/ A jug of wine, a loaf of bread, and thou"—Omar Khayyam). The remaining toasts are anonymous.

HERE'S TO FLEXIBILITY

- Feel free to personalize your toast. If the toast starts out with "To him," "To her," "To the man," "To our professor," or "To our host," substitute "To Megan," "To Matthew," or "To Mr. Slate-Greene."

- Have fun. These toasts aren't set in stone. Modify them any way you wish. For example, "May you die in bed at age ninety-five shot by the jealous husband of a teenage wife." "AGE," (page 10) can be easily switched to: "May you die in bed at age ninety-five shot by the jealous wife of a teenage husband."

THE PRICE OF SUCCESS

This book gives you all the material you need to give crisp, witty toasts. If, however, you get a reputation for giving clever and amusing toasts, you'll probably get invited to participate in a roast or give a speech. To prepare for those occasions, you'll want to pick up a copy of *Well-Done Roasts*—Witty Insults, Quips & Wisecracks Perfect for Every Imaginable Occasion or *And I Quote*—The Definitive Collection of Quotes, Sayings & Jokes for the Contemporary Speech-Maker. Both are published by St. Martin's Press.

Crisp Toasts

ABSENT FRIENDS

- Here's to our absent friends—in the hopes that they, wherever they are, are drinking to us.

- "Oh, here's to other meetings,
  And merry greetings then,
  And here's to those we've drunk with,
  But never can again."
  —Stephen Decatur

- Here's to absent friends—particularly to prosperity.

- Here's to our faraway friends. May their spirits be with us as soon as these spirits are in us.

- To our absent friends. Although they are out of sight, we recognize them with our glasses.

- Here's to our absent friends—God bless them.

- Here's to absent friends—both the long-lost friends of our youth and our long-lost youth.

- Here's to the woman I love,
  I wish that she were nigh;
  If drinking beer would bring her here,
  I'd drink the damned place dry.

- Here's to the girl I love best,
  I picked her out from all the rest;
  She's not here to take her part,
  So I'll drink to her with all my heart.

ACCOUNTANTS

- To my accountant—may he make many brilliant deductions.

- Here's to our accountant—if we had royalty in America, he'd surely be a Count.

- Here's to the accountant—the person who tells you what to do with your money after you've done something else with it.

- To accountants—the people who really know the score in business.

ACTION

- Here's to doing and drinking, not sitting and thinking.

- May we always have the class
  To rise and get up off our ass.
  When there are deeds that must be done
  Or novel ways to have fun.

- To quote the Nike ad campaign, "Just Do It."

- "The harder you work, the luckier you get."
  —Gary Player

- To quote from the movie *Risky Business*, "Sometimes you've just got to say, 'What the fuck . . .'"

- May we be known by our deeds, not by our mortgages.

- To action. As Benjamin Disraeli said, "Action may not always bring happiness, but there is no happiness without action."

- Here's to action. In the words of George Bernard Shaw, "You don't learn to hold your own in the world by standing on guard, but by attacking and getting well hammered yourself."

- To protest—may we never fail to rise up when the government falls down.

- Here's to those who have had the courage to speak out. They alone have served truth. As Henri Frédéric Amiel said, "Truth is not only violated by falsehood; it may be equally outraged by silence."

ADOLESCENCE

- To adolescence—that period when children refuse to believe that someday they'll be as dumb as their parents.

- To adolescence—that period when children feel their parents should be told the facts of life.

- To our adolescent friends. May their characters grow as fast as their bodies.

- Here's to our adolescent friends. May their clothes never be as loud as their music.

- To the surging confusion caused by love and hormones—may we always feel it.

ADVENTURE

- "A health to the man on the trail tonight; may his grub hold out; may his dogs keep their legs; may his matches never misfire."
  —Jack London

- To Kurt Vonnegut, who said, "Unusual travel suggestions are dancing lessons from the gods."

- As Mikey said in the Life cereal commercials, "Try it. You'll like it."

- "A pledge from heart to its fellow heart
  On the ways we all are going!
  Here's luck!
  For we know not where we are going."
  —Richard Hovey

- Here's to you and here's to me,
  Wherever we may roam;
  And here's to the health and happiness
  Of the ones who are left at home.

- "Wealth I ask not, hope nor love,
  Nor a friend to know me,
  All I ask is the heav'n above,
  And the roads below me!"
  —Robert Louis Stevenson

- Take a trail, good friend. And luck to you.

ADVERSITY

- Clink, clink your glasses and drink;
  Why should we trouble borrow?
  Care not for sorrow,
  A fig for the morrow.
  Tonight let's be merry and drink.

- You shall and you shan't,
  You will and you won't,
  You're condemned if you do,

4

And you're damned if you don't.
So let's drink!

- 'Tis easy to say "Fill 'em"
  When your account's not overdrawn.
  But the man worthwhile,
  Is the man who can smile,
  When every damned cent is gone.

- To the difficulties that we have encountered, in acknowledgment of the fact that they have made us stronger.

- Don't let the bastards grind you down.

- If the world is going wrong,
  Forget it!
  Sorrow never lingers long—
  Forget it!
  If your neighbor bears ill-will,
  If your conscience won't be still,
  If you owe an ancient bill,
  Forget it!

- Laugh and the world laughs with you,
  Weep, and it gives you the laugh anyway.

- May the sunshine of comfort shine through the gloom of despair.

- Here's to absent friends—particularly to prosperity.

- It's not as bad a world
  As some would like to make it;
  But whether it's good or bad,
  Depends on how you take it.

- "Within this goblet, rich and deep,
  I cradle all my woes to sleep."
  —Tom Moore

- To quote Richard Stillman Powell,
  "Now, down with care and blithely swear
  A truce to melancholy;
  Let each good soul fill up his bowl
  And drink a toast to folly."

- "Fill up the bowl, upon my soul,
  Your trouble you'll forget, sir;
  If it takes more, fill twenty score,
  Till you have drowned regret, sir."
  —Alfred Brenn

- To better days—may the happiest days of your past be the saddest days of your future.

- May the sunshine of hope dispel calamity's clouds.

- Here's to the pressure we face—for it is, after all, pressure that turns coal into diamonds.

- As Shakespeare said in *The Merry Wives of Windsor*, let us "Drink down all unkindness."

- A speedy calm to the storms of life.

- Here's to you, my honest friend,
  Wishing these hard times to mend.

- May the frowns of misfortune never rob innocence of its joy.

- Here's to the fellow who smiles
  When life rolls along like a song,
  And here's to the chap who can smile
  When everything goes dead wrong.

- To our troubles and to our inevitable victory. As Seneca said, "Fire is the test of gold; adversity of strong men."

- To adversity. In the words of George Bernard Shaw, "You don't learn to hold your own in the world by standing on guard, but by attacking and getting well hammered yourself."

ADVERTISING

- To advertising, which Marshall McLuhan called "the greatest art form of the twentieth century."

- Here's to advertising. As Stuart Henderson Britt said, "Doing business without advertising is like winking at a girl in the dark. You know what you are doing, but nobody else does."

- To big budgets. In the words of P. T. Barnum, "Advertising is like learning—a little is a dangerous thing."

- Here's to H. L. Mencken, who said, "No one ever went broke underestimating the taste of the American public."

- Here's to the mints—the only places that make money without advertising.

ADVICE

- Here are some words to live by: Love to one, friendship to many, and goodwill to all.

- May you live to learn well, and learn to live well.

- Here's to the wisdom of all who come to us for advice.

- Good, better, best;
  Never let it rest,
  Till your good is better,
  And your better best.

- Do not resist growing old—many are denied the privilege.

- To quote from the lyrics of "The Ballad of Captain Kidd,"
  "Take warning now by me,

And shun bad company,
Lest you come to hell with me."

- To the wise women here tonight, a word of advice: distrust men in general, but not us in particular.

AGE

Middle Age

- To our favorite old hippie. Let me assure you that this is a real celebration, and not an acid flashback.

- To middle age, which Don Marquis once described as "the time when a man is always thinking that in a week or two he will feel as good as ever."

- In the words of Ben Jonson,
  "To the old, long life and treasure;
  To the young, all health and pleasure."

- To the most closely guarded secret in this country—your real age.

- To middle age, when we begin to exchange our emotions for symptoms.

- To our friend who is aging wonderfully. Nothing about you is old, except a few of your jokes.

- Here's to a man who's discovered what really separates the men from the boys—many years.

- To Europe, where they believe that women get more attractive after thirty-five.

- To age. In the words of Frank Lloyd Wright, "The longer I live, the more beautiful life becomes."

- Here's to absent friends—both the long-lost friends of our youth and our long-lost youth.

- May your fire never go out.

- May your well never run dry.

- May the Lord love us but not call us too soon.

- May time never turn your head gray.

- You're not as young as you used to be, but you're not as old as you're going to be—so watch it!

- To wine. It improves with age—I like it more the older I get.

- Here's to you! No matter how old you are, you don't look it.

Old Age

- "Old wood to burn, old wine to drink, old friends to trust, and old authors to read."
  —Francis Bacon

- May the clouds in your life be only a background for a lovely sunset.

- In the words of Oliver Goldsmith, "I love everything that's old—old friends, old times, old manners, old books, old wine."

- May you live to be a hundred years with one extra year to repent.

- Do not resist growing old—many are denied the privilege.

- Here's a health to the future;
  A sigh for the past;
  We can love and remember,
  And hope to the last.

And for all the base lies
That the almanacs hold,
While there's love in the heart,
We can never grow old.

- In the words of Larry E. Johnson,
  "May our lives, like the leaves of the maple, grow
  More beautiful as they fade.
  May we say our farewells, when it's time to go,
  All smiling and unafraid."

- May you live to be a hundred—and decide the rest for yourself.

- Here's to you: May you live as long as you want to. May you want to as long as you live.

- To old age, may it always be ten years older than I am.

- To the "metallic" age—gold in our teeth, silver in our hair, and lead in our pants.

- May the pleasures of youth never bring us pain in old age.

- To old age, or as William Allen White said on his seventieth birthday, "I am not afraid of tomorrow, for I have seen yesterday and I love today."

- To old age—it's not how old you are, but how you are old.

- To my old friend. As Marjorie Barstow Breenbie once said, "Beautiful young people are accidents of nature. But beautiful old people are works of art."

- May you die in bed at age ninety-five shot by the jealous husband of a teenage wife.

- May you enter heaven late.

- The good die young—here's hoping you live to a ripe old age.

- May you live to be as old as your jokes.

- To my old cronies—may they never be too old to be young.

- May we keep a little of the fuel of youth to warm our body in old age.

- May we live to learn well, and learn to live well.

- May we never do worse.

- May we never feel want, nor ever want feeling.

AMBITION

- Here's to great ambition,
  About which people rant.
  It makes you want to do the things
  That everyone knows you can't.

- To a man who is a true inspiration to the rest of us. If you can make it, surely we can, too.

- Good, better, best;
  Never let it rest,
  Till your good is better,
  And your better best.

- To the desire to triumph. In the words of Vince Lombardi, "Winning isn't everything—but wanting to win is."

- Here's to our trying. As the saying goes, "Nothing ventured, nothing gained."

- To our daring. As they say, "No guts, no glory."

- To giant steps, because, as David Lloyd George said, "The most dangerous thing in the world is to leap a chasm in two jumps."

AMERICA

- To the United States of America. We may have our critics, but, as the saying goes, "Immigration is the sincerest form of flattery."

- May we always remember what red, white, and blue really stand for—love, purity, and fidelity.

- Here's a health to America, the pride of the earth,
  The Stars and the Stripes—drink the land of our birth!
  Toast the army and navy who fought for our cause,
  Who conquered and won us our freedom and laws.

- May every patriot love his country, whether he was born in it or not.

- Here's to America, or in the words of Oliver Wendell Holmes, "One flag, one land, one heart, one hand, one nation evermore."

- Here's to America. In the words of Stephen Decatur, ". . . our country right or wrong."

- To America. As Carl Schurz once said, "Our country! When right, to be kept right. When wrong, to be put right!"

- To the land we love, and the love we land.

- May the seeds of dissension never find growth in the soil of America.

- To the land we live in, love, and would die for.

- Here's to the army and navy,
  And the battles they have won,
  Here's to America's colors—
  The colors that never run.

- The union of lakes, the union of lands,
  The union of states none can sever;

The union of hearts, the union of hands,
And the flag of our union forever.

- To the United States, where each man is protected by the Constitution regardless of whether he has ever taken the time to read it.

- In the words of David Starr Jordan, "Rome endured as long as there were Romans. Americans will endure as long as we remain American in spirit and thought."

- To America, may we always be, as Omar Bradley said, "an arsenal of hope."

- Here's to America and England. In the words of Charles Dickens, "May they never have any division but the Atlantic between them."

- Here's to America and England. To quote George Bernard Shaw, here's to "two countries separated by the same language."

- To America—may we never lose sight of the fact that we are, in the words of Adlai Stevenson, "the first community in which men set out to institutionalize freedom, responsible government, and human equality."

- Here's to the American Eagle—the liberty bird that permits no unjust liberties.

- We've toasted all names and all places,
  We've toasted all kinds of game,
  Why not just for loyalty's sake
  Drink one to our nation's name.

- "To her we drink, for her we pray,
  Our voices silent never;
  For her we'll fight, come what may,
  The Stars and Stripes forever."
  —Stephen Decatur

- The Lily of France may fade,
  The Thistle and Shamrock wither,
  The Oak of England may decay,
  But the Stars shine on forever.

- America! my country, great and free.
  Heart of the world, I drink to thee.

- To America. Let us always remember that the last two syllables of American are "I CAN."

- The Frenchman loves his native wine;
  The German loves his beer;
  The Englishman loves his 'alf and 'alf,
  Because it brings good cheer.
  The Irishman loves his whisky straight,
  Because it gives him dizziness.
  The American has no choice at all,
  So he drinks the whole damned business.

ANNIVERSARY

- Here's to the husband—
  And here's to the wife;
  May they remain
  Lovers for life.

- May their joys be as deep as the ocean
  And their misfortunes as light as the foam.

- May you grow old on one pillow.

- May your love be as endless as your wedding rings.

- To my spouse:
  Here's a health to the future,

A sigh for the past,
We can love and remember
And love to the last.

- To my wife and our anniversary, which I forgot once, but will never forget again.

- Here's to you both—
A beautiful pair,
On the birthday of
Your love affair.

- To the happy couple. Let anniversaries come and let anniversaries go—but may your happiness continue on forever.

- To your coming anniversaries—may they be outnumbered only by your coming pleasures.

- To my spouse:
Because I love you truly,
Because you love me, too,
My very greatest happiness
Is sharing life with you.

- To a couple so happy they raise the same question in all of our minds—"Are you sure they're married?"

- To my parents' anniversary—that most important day, which proves that I am, after all, legitimate.

APRIL FOOLS' DAY

- "Let us toast the fools; but for them, the rest of us could not succeed."
—Mark Twain

- To April Fools' Day—the most honest day of the year.

- May the skepticism that we develop on April Fools' Day protect us for the rest of the year.

- May the jokes we fall for today be the only ones we fall for all year.

ARCHITECTS

- To the architect—she's lucky we finished the job before the building inspector came around.

- Here's to the travails of being an architect. To quote Frank Lloyd Wright, "The physician can bury his mistakes, but the architect can only advise his client to plant vines."

- To the architect—in the immortal words of Ambrose Bierce, "one who drafts a plan of your house, and plans a draft of your money."

- As we architects love to say, "Back to the drawing board."

- Here's to the ivy that eventually covers our mistakes.

ART

- Here's to art. As G. K. Chesterton once said so eloquently, "Art, like morality, consists in drawing the line somewhere."

- To art. As George Bernard Shaw said, "Without art, the crudeness of reality would make the world unbearable."

- To art—that which distinguishes man from beast.

- To art—may we all serve it.

- To art, which demands all our energy—or to quote Ralph Waldo Emerson, "Art is a jealous mistress."

- Ben Jonson said, "Art has an enemy called ignorance." Here's to the triumph of art and the end to ignorance.

- As Victor Cousin said, "Art for art's sake."

ARTISTS

- To the artist. To quote John O'Hara, "An artist is his own fault."

- Let's lift our glasses to the artist, who has just completed a lovely painting—and missed none of the numbers!

- Here's to the artist. In the words of Robert W. Corrigan, "The artist is the seismograph of his age."

- To the artist. Havelock Ellis said it best when he said, "Every artist writes his own autobiography."

ATHLETES

- To those whose bodies are temples—may you never build an unwanted addition.

- May you enjoy the three skills of the hare: sharp turning, high jumping, and strong running against the hill.

- To our favorite swinger—may he always play the field and never be caught off base.

- Here's to all those true competitors, or in the immortal words of Vince Lombardi, "Winning isn't everything—but wanting to win is."

- To a real nice guy and the ultimate athlete. He's the only one I know who disproves Leo Durocher's famous quote, "Nice guys finish last."

- May we build muscles everywhere but in our heads.

BACHELORS & BACHELORETTES

- Woman—the morning star of infancy, the day star of manhood, the evening star of old age; bless our stars and may they always be kept at a telescopic distance.

- To the bachelor—a man who prefers to ball without the chain.

- 'Tis better to have loved and lost,
  Than to marry and be bossed.

- Drink, my buddies, drink with discerning,
  Wedlock's lane where there is no turning;
  Never was owl more blind than lover;
  Drink and be merry, lads; and think it over.

- Say it with flowers
  Say it with eats,
  Say it with kisses,
  Say it with sweets,
  Say it with jewelry,
  Say it with drink,
  But always be careful
  Not to say it with ink.

- Here's to the bachelorette—she looks but she won't leap.

- To the bachelor, a man who refuses to play troth or consequences.

- To the bachelorette, a woman who hasn't made the same mistake once.

- To the bachelor, a man who can have a girl on his knees without having her on his hands.

- Here's to the bachelorette, a woman who won't take yes for an answer.

- To the bachelor, who, as Helen Rowland once remarked, "never quite gets over the idea that he is a thing of beauty and a boy forever."

- To the wisdom of the bachelor. To quote H. L. Mencken, he "knows more about women than married men; if he didn't, he'd be married too."

- "Marriage is a wonderful institution, but who wants to live in an institution?"
  —Groucho Marx

- Needles and pins, needles and pins
  When a man marries his troubles begin.

- In the words of Minna Thomas Antrim,
  "Drink, for who knows when Cupid's arrow keen,
  Shall strike us and no more we'll here be seen."

- To men—the bitter half of women.

- To the bachelors—may they never impale their freedom upon the point of a pen.

- A game, a book, a fire, a friend,
  A beer that's always full,
  Here's to the joys of a bachelor's life,
  A life that's never dull.

BALDNESS

- Here's to our bald friend, whose head resembles heaven—"there is no parting there."

- To our bald friend, whose head is a shining example!

- To baldness—the proof of the old saying "Hair today, gone tomorrow."

- To those who let no hair come between them and higher wisdom.

BANKERS

- Here's to the banks. To quote Mark Twain, "Banks will lend you money if you can prove you don't need it."

- To the banker—a person who lends you an umbrella on a fair day only to take it away when it rains.

- Here's to the banker—the man behind most self-made men.

- To our misguided friend the banker, who thought he was going into a simple, stable profession.

- To our friend the banker—may he never lose interest.

BEAUTY

- To beauty, or in the words of Charles Kingsley, "Never lose an opportunity of seeing anything beautiful. Beauty is God's handwriting."

- Every day you look lovelier and lovelier—and today you look like tomorrow.

- To quote John Keats's immortal line, "A thing of beauty is a joy forever." Here's to you, beautiful.

- Here's to our gorgeous friend, who has proved that a beautiful flower can arise from a heap of manure.

BEER

- In the words of the old ballad,
  "He that drinketh strong beer and goes to bed right mellow,
  Lives as he ought to live and dies a hearty fellow."

- O thrice accursed
  Be a champagne thirst
  When the price of beer's all we've got.

- Let's drink the liquid of amber so bright;
  Let's drink the liquid with foam snowy white;
  Let's drink the liquid that brings all good cheer;
  Oh, where is the drink like old-fashioned beer?

- W. L. Hassoldt said it best:
  "None so deaf as those who will not hear.
  None so blind as those who will not see.
  But I'll wager none so deaf nor blind that he
  Sees not nor hears me say come drink this beer."

- Who'd care to be a bee and sip
  Sweet honey from the flower's lip
  When he might be a fly and steer
  Head first into a can of beer?

- Such power hath beer.
  The heart where
  Grief hath cankered
  Hath one unfailing remedy—the tankard.

- Here's to the heavenly brew. As they say at Otter Creek Brewing, Middlebury, Vermont, "For a quart of ale is dish for a king."
- 'Twas ever thus from childhood's hour,
  I've seen my fond hopes disappear;
  I've always had a champagne thirst,
  But have to be content with beer.

BENEFACTORS

- To a person so generous that it makes me want to say, "Yes, my friends, there is a Santa Claus."
- To our benefactor, whose presents make our hearts grow fonder.
- Here's to our benefactor, who is to be honored. As Calvin Coolidge said, "No person was ever honored for what he received. Honor has been the reward for what he gave."
- To quote Jonathan Brown, "Whenever the occasion arose, he rose to the occasion."
- To our benefactor—who came forward when we needed him most, proving the old saying that "When it gets dark enough, you will see the stars."
- To our good friend and benefactor, whose charity never failed us.
- Here's to our benefactor, whom God must love, for the Bible says, "God loveth a cheerful giver."

BEST WISHES

- In the words of *Star Trek*'s Mr. Spock, "Live long and prosper."
- "Here's to your good health, and your family's good health, and may you all live long and prosper."
  —Washington Irving

- May you live as long as you want to and may you want to as long as you live.

- May your fire never go out.

- May your well never run dry.

- May the Lord love us but not call us too soon.

- May you live to be a hundred years with one extra year to repent.

- Long life to you and may you die in your bed.

- May your enemies never meet a friend.

- May the saints protect you, and sorrow neglect you, and bad luck to the one that doesn't respect you.

- May you live to be a hundred—and decide the rest for yourself.

- May time never turn your head gray.

- "Were't the last drop in the well,
  An I gasp'd upon the brink,
  Ere my fainting spirit fell,
  'Tis to thee that I would drink."
  —Lord Byron

- May we never grumble without cause, and may we never have cause to grumble.

- May we live respected and die regretted.

- May your voyage through life be as happy and as free
  As the dancing waves on the deep blue sea.

- May you be hung, drawn and quartered—
  Hung in the hall of fame,
  Drawn by a golden chariot,
  And quartered in the arms of the one you love best.

- May we each offer: love to one, friendship to many, and goodwill to all.

- May the most you wish for be the least you get.

- As you slide down the banister of life, may the splinters never face the wrong way.

- Here's to turkey when you're hungry,
  Champagne when you are dry,
  A great lover when you need one,
  And heaven when you die.

- May the road rise to meet you.
  May the wind be always at your back,
  The sun shine warm upon your face,
  The rain fall soft upon your fields,
  And until we meet again
  May God hold you in the hollow of his hand.

- May each of us be what he or she wants to be.

- May poverty always be a day's march behind us.

- All the best to you, from one who remembers when you were an immature brat . . . last week.

- To quote from Shakespeare's *Henry VIII*, "A health, gentlemen, Let it go round."

- As Shakespeare said in *The Merchant of Venice*, "I wish you all the joy you can wish."

- May bad fortune follow you all of your days—and never catch up with you!

- I wish you all the best. As Shakespeare said in *Timon of Athens*, may "the best of happiness, honor and fortunes keep with you."

- When we are right, may it be long remembered. When we are wrong, may it be soon forgotten.

- May we never speak to deceive nor listen to betray.

- May we never know want until relief is at hand.

- May you die in bed at age ninety-five shot by the jealous husband of a teenage wife.

- May you enter heaven late.

- May the saints protect you,
  And sorrow neglect you,
  And bad luck to the one
  That doesn't respect you.

BIBLICAL

- Where there is no vision, the people perish. —Proverbs 29:18

- The truth shall make you free. —John 8:32

- Eat thy bread with joy, and drink thy wine with a merry heart. —Ecclesiastes 9:7

- Forsake not an old friend, for the new is not comparable to him. A new friend is as new wine: when it is old, thou shalt drink it with pleasure. —Ecclesiasticus 9:10

- The best wine . . . goeth down sweetly, causing the lips of those that are asleep to speak. —Song of Solomon 7:9

- Wine was created from the beginning to make men joyful, and not to make men drunk. Wine drunk with moderation is the joy of the soul and the heart. —Ecclesiasticus 31:27–28

- To eat, to drink, and be merry. —Ecclesiastes 8:15

- Let us eat and drink: for tomorrow we shall die. —Isaiah 22:13

- A feast is made for laughter, and wine maketh merry. —Ecclesiastes 10:19

- Drink no longer water, but use a little wine for thy stomach's sake.—1 Timothy 5:23

- Give . . . wine unto those that be of heavy heart. —Proverbs 31:6

- Wine maketh glad the hearts of man. —Psalms 104:15

- Wine, which cheereth gods and men. —Judges 9:13

- As we have therefore opportunity, let us do good unto all men. —Galatians 6:10

BIRTHDAY

- Another candle on your cake?
  Well, that's no cause to pout.
  Be glad that you have strength enough
  To blow the damn thing out.

- Another year older?
  Think this way:
  Just one day older
  Than yesterday.

- Happy birthday to you
  And many to be,
  With friends that are true
  As you are to me.

- Here's to you! No matter how old you are, you don't look it.

- In the words of Robert H. Lord,
  "Many happy returns of the day of your birth:
  Many blessings to brighten your pathway on earth;

Many friendships to cheer and provoke you to mirth;
Many feastings and frolics to add to your girth."

- May you live to be a hundred years with one extra year to repent.

- We wish you joy on your birthday
And all the whole year through,
For all the best that life can hold
Is none too good for you.

- To the birthday girl—how am I to remember your birthday when you never look any older?

- To the most closely guarded secret in this country, your real age.

- I raise my glass to say,
It's your birthday, that's true;
And to celebrate the fact
That I'm younger than you.

- To fine traditions—like birthday spankings!

- To a person who has matured, so that she no longer shouts "Go for it," but now calmly says, "Have it delivered."

- Although another year is past
He seems no older than the last!

- Time marches on
Now tell the truth—
Where did you find
The fountain of youth?

- To your birthday, glass held high,
Glad it's you that's older—not I.

BOSSES

- To our boss—the star to which we have all hitched our wagon.

- Here's to the man who signs our paychecks—may he never hear what we say about him.

27

- To the boss—the person who's early when you're late, and late when you're early.

- May we never flatter our superiors or insult our inferiors.

- Here's to bosses and diapers—both are always on your ass and usually full of shit.

- Here's to our boss. When he tells you not to worry—start worrying.

BRIDES & GROOMS

- Here's to the bride and the bridegroom,
  We'll ask their success in our prayers,
  And through life's dark shadows and sunshine
  That good luck may always be theirs.

- Here's to thee and thy folks from me and my folks;
  And if thee and thy folks love me and my folks
  As much as me and my folks love thee and thy folks
  Then there never was folks since folks was folks
  Love me and my folks as much as thee and thy folks.

- In the immortal words of Ralph Waldo Emerson, "Here's to the happy man: All the world loves a lover."

- Here's to the groom with bride so fair,
  And here's to the bride with groom so rare!

- To the man who has conquered the bride's heart, and her mother's.

- Here's to the new husband—and here's to the new wife;
  May they remain lovers for all of life.

- Here's to the bride and the groom!
  May you have a happy honeymoon,

May you lead a happy life,
May you make a bunch of money soon,
And live without all strife.

- Here's to the bride. Anna Lewis said it best when she wrote,
"Love, be true to her; Life, be dear to her;
Health, stay close to her; Joy, draw near to her;
Fortune, find what you can do for her,
Search your treasure-house through and through for her,
Follow her footsteps the wide world over—
And keep her husband always her lover."

- Here's to the bride—may your hours of joy be as numerous
as the petals of your bridal bouquet.

- Here's to our groom—a man who keeps his head though he
loses his heart.

- Here's to the man whose best girl is his mother, and whose
sweetheart is his wife.

- A toast to the groom—and discretion to his bachelor friends.

BROTHERS

- To the *r* in the word brother—without it, you'd just be a
bother.

- To the man who's really happy he has an older brother—can
you imagine how he'd look in his sister's hand-me-downs?

- Here's to the bond that comes from having the same parents.

- To my brother. As John Ray said, "Blood is thicker than
water."

BUILDERS

- Here's to the man who comes home every day and says his work was riveting.
- To building—the profession where you always start in the hole.
- Here's to the heroes who make our homes.
- To the brotherhood of hammer and saw.

BUSINESS

- To all the pleasures that other people's money pays for.
- To goodwill, which Marshall Field called, "the one and only asset that competition cannot undersell or destroy."
- May we always be fired with enthusiasm for our work, and never fired enthusiastically by our clients.
- To the entrepreneur—he knows money doesn't talk nowadays, it goes without saying.
- To the company we keep profitable.
- To Calvin Coolidge, the man who said, "The business of America is business."
- To the thing that has made America great—free commerce.

CELEBRATION

- In the words of Bill and Ted, "Party on, dudes" and "Be excellent to each other."
- Eat thy bread with joy, and drink thy wine with a merry heart. —Ecclesiastes 9:7

- Drink and be merry, for our time on earth is short, and death lasts forever.

- To the good old days—which we are having right now.

- As Baba Meher said, "Don't worry, be happy."

- After everything that has happened, I can only quote the last words of Czar Alexander I of Russia: "What a beautiful day."

- "Drink today and drown all sorrow,
  You shall perhaps not do't tomorrow.
  Best while you have it, use your breath;
  There is no drinking after death."
  —Francis Beaumont and John Fletcher

CHAMPAGNE

- The miser may be pleased with gold,
  The lady's man with pretty lass;
  But I'm best pleased when I behold
  The nectar sparkling in the glass.

- To champagne—a beverage that makes you see double and feel single.

- Here's to champagne, a drink divine
  That makes us forget our troubles;
  It's made of a dollar's worth of wine,
  And twenty bucks worth of bubbles.

- O thrice accursed
  Be a champagne thirst
  When the price of beer's all we've got.

- To champagne—
  Nectar strained to finest gold,
  Sweet as love, as virtue cold.

- Here's champagne to our real friends and real pain to our sham friends.

- "Some take their gold
  In minted mold,
  And some in harps hereafter,
  But give me mine
  In bubbles fine
  And keep the change in laughter."
  —Oliver Herford

- May we always be as bubbly as this champagne.

CHARITY

- To the best of all nations—donation.

- To a person so generous that it makes me want to say, "Yes, my friends, there is a Santa Claus."

- As we have therefore opportunity, let us do good unto all men. —Galatians 6:10

- May the heart that melts at the sight of sorrow always be blessed with the means to relieve it.

- Here's riches to the generous and power to the merciful.

- May we strengthen the weak,
  Give light to the blind,
  Clothe the naked,
  And be friends to mankind.

- Here's to those of us who work for charity—we have to, nobody will pay us.

- To charity—unless a man is a recipient of charity, he should be a contributor to it.

- In the words of Alexander Pope,
"In faith and hope the world will disagree,
But all mankind's concern is charity."

- To our benefactor, a person, in the words of Chauncey Depew, "who makes two smiles grow where one grew before."

- The best way I can think of to ask for your support is to use the words that the famous suffragette Lucy Stone chose for her last words: "Make the world better."

- In the words of Josh Billings, "Remember the poor—it costs nothing."

- As Francis Bacon said, "In charity there is no excess."

- To the spirit of charity. As Clint W. Murchison said, "Money is like manure. If you spread it around, it does a lot of good, but if you pile it up in one place, it stinks like hell."

CHILDREN

- To the new parents, who are about to enter a "changing" world!

- A generation of children on the children of your children.

- To our children, and let us not forget, as Joseph Joubert said, that they "have more need of models than of critics."

- To your newborn—an alimentary canal with a loud noise at one end and no responsibility at the other.

- As Dorothy Parker once said to a friend who had just given birth, "Congratulations: we all knew you had it in you."

- To children—the future of the world.

- Here's to children—the truest legacy we leave to the world.

- To the children of the world—may they never go hungry.

- To children—may we be patient with their questions.

- To the innocence of children and the inner sense of adults.

- A new life begun,
  Like father, like son.

- Like one, like the other,
  Like daughter, like mother.

- Here's to the baby—man to be—
  May he be as fine as thee.

- Here's to the baby—woman to be—
  May she be as sweet as thee.

- May your baby grow twice as tall as yourself and half as wise.

- "Every baby born into the world is a finer one than the last."
  —Charles Dickens

- "We haven't all had the good fortune to be ladies, we haven't all been generals or poets or statesmen; but when the toast works down to babies, we stand on common ground."
  —Mark Twain

- To babies—they will make love stronger, days shorter, nights longer, bankrolls smaller, home happier, clothes shabbier, the past forgotten, and the future worth living for.

- To the new parents. They will learn, as I did, about babies, that you've got to love them. Unfortunately, you also have to feed them and change them, too. Good luck.

- To the new baby, who, as the parents will soon find out, is the perfect example of minority rule.

- May you have many children; and may they grow as mature in taste, and as healthy in color, and as sought after as the contents of this glass.

- As they say in the diaper business, bottoms up.

- Here's to my child. Someone I've known for his whole life, who, nonetheless, continues to surprise and impress me.

CHRISTENING

- May this be the last bath at which your baby cries.

- In the words of Charles Dickens, "Every baby born into the world is a finer one than the last."

- A baby will make love stronger, days shorter, nights longer, bankroll smaller, home happier, clothes shabbier, the past forgotten, and the future worth living for.

- A new life begun,
  Like father, like son.

- Like one, like the other,
  Like daughter, like mother.

- Here's to the baby—man to be—
  May he be as fine as thee.

- Here's to baby—woman to be—
  May she be as sweet as thee.

CHRISTMAS

- I know I've wished you this before
  But every year I wish it more.
  A Merry Christmas.

- To Christmas—hang up love's mistletoe over the earth, and let us kiss under it all the year round.

- A Christmas wish—may you never forget what is worth remembering or remember what is best forgotten.

- Be merry all, be merry all,
  With holly dress the festive hall,
  Prepare the song, the feast, the ball,
  To welcome Merry Christmas.

- To a person so generous that it makes me want to say, "Yes, my friends, there is a Santa Claus."

- In the immortal words of Tiny Tim in Charles Dickens's *A Christmas Carol*, "Here's to us all! God bless us every one!"

- "Christmas . . .
  A day when cheer and gladness blend,
  When heart meets heart
  And friend meets friend."
  —J. H. Fairweather

- I wish you a Merry Christmas
  And a Happy New Year,
  A pocket full of money
  And a cooler full of beer.

- May yours be the first house in the city to welcome St. Nicholas.

- Here's to the white of the mistletoe,
  And to its many leaves so green;
  And here's to the lips of ruby red,
  Waiting 'neath to complete the scene.

- Here's to friends we've yet to meet,
  Here's to those here; all here I greet;
  Here's to childhood, youth, old age,
  Here's to prophet, bard and sage,
  Here's to your health—may all be bright
  On this so special Christmas night.

- "At Christmas play and make good cheer
  For Christmas comes but once a year."
  —Thomas Turner

- Here's to the holly with its bright red berry.
  Here's to Christmas, let's make it merry.

- Here's wishing you more happiness
  Than all my words can tell,
  Not just alone for Christmas
  But for all the year as well.

CLERGY

- To our minister—who would rather preach than practice.

- To our pastor and his divine influence. As Minister Harry Emerson Fosdick once said, "Preaching is personal counseling on a group basis."

- To the Padre who by not drinking leaves more for us.

- Here's to our priest. In the words of Robert Runcie, former archbishop of Canterbury, "The priest is concerned with other people for the sake of God and with God for the sake of other people."

- Here's to the Messengers of Peace.

COACHES

- Here's to the man who made us winners.

- Here's to our coach—a man who's willing to lay down our lives for his school.

- To the man for whom sweat is sweet.

- Let's drink to the coach—and hope he doesn't catch us!

- Here's to the woman who taught us the meaning of Vince Lombardi's saying: "Winning isn't everything—but wanting to win is."

COFFEE

- To strong, hot coffee—
  It's what I'll take
  Tomorrow morning
  For my headache.

- To coffee—
  Black as the devil,
  Strong as death,
  Sweet as love, and
  Hot as hell!

- To a hot, steaming cup of Joe
  Tomorrow when I wake up slow.

- To coffee—
  Life would truly be obscene
  Without occasional caffeine.

COURAGE

- Here's to you from morning till night;
  Here's to the person with courage to fight—
  The courage to fight and the courage to live—
  The courage to learn, and to love, and forgive.

- To quote Victor Hugo, "If we must suffer, let us suffer nobly."
- To courage, which Ernest Hemingway defined as "grace under pressure."
- Here's to our brave forefathers. As Jonathan Swift said, "He was a bold man that first ate an oyster."
- In the immortal words of John Paul Jones, "I have not yet begun to fight."
- May noise never excite us to battle, or confusion reduce us to defeat.

COUSINS

- To my cousins—because of you, I never felt like an only child.
- Here's to cousins—kissing and otherwise.
- To our clan
  The best there are
  Every woman
  Every man.
- To my many cousins, who always made it seem that everything is relative.
- To my overseas cousins. As John Ray said, "Blood is thicker than water."

CREDIT & CREDITORS

- Here's to the creditor—long may he waive.
- May the weight of our taxes never bend the back of our credit.
- Here's to our creditors—may they be endowed with the four assets, faith, hope, charity, and Alzheimer's.

CRITICS

- Here's to a good critic who, as Anatole France said, "relates the adventures of his soul among masterpieces."

- To the critic—someone who likes to write about things he doesn't like.

- To our critics I offer the wise words of Benjamin Disraeli, who said, "It is much easier to be critical than to be correct."

- To our critics I give the words of Rudolf Bing, who said, "I am perfectly happy to believe that nobody likes us but the public."

- To the critics' patron saint, Harry S. Truman, to whom these immortal words are attributed: "If you can't stand the heat, you'd better get out of the kitchen."

CURSES

- Here's to short shoes and long corns for our enemies.

- May a band of gypsies camp in your belly and train bears to dance on your liver.

- May the devil cut the toes off all our foes, that we may know them by their limping.

- May the devil make a ladder of your backbone while he is picking apples in the garden of hell.

- May you turn into a sparrow and owe your existence to the droppings of a horse.

- May all your teeth fall out—but one should remain for a toothache.

DEAR DEPARTED

- To our dear departed friend—Oliver Herford was right: "Only the good die young."

- "Let us make our glasses kiss;
  Let us quench the sorrow-cinders."
  —Ralph Waldo Emerson

- May every hair on your head turn into a candle to light your way to heaven, and may God and his Holy Mother take the harm of the years away from you.

- "Oh, here's to other meetings,
  And merry greetings then;
  And here's to those we've drunk with.
  But never can again."
  —Stephen Decatur

- Time cuts down all,
  Both great and small.

- To live in hearts we leave behind, is not to die.

- To our dear departed, that the devil mightn't hear of his death, till he's safe inside the walls of heaven.

- "Now let us sit and drink and make us merry,
  And afterward we will his body bury."
  —Geoffrey Chaucer

- Here's to the tears of affection,
  May they crystallize as they fall,
  And become pearls, that in the after years
  We'll wear in memory of those whom we have loved.

- To our loved ones who have passed away, may the winds of heaven whisper hourly benedictions over their hallowed graves.

41

- "I hold it true, whate'er befall,
  I feel it when I sorrow most;
  'Tis better to have loved and lost,
  Than never to have loved at all."
  —Alfred, Lord Tennyson

DEDICATION

- To the power of the human spirit. In the words of William Faulkner, "I believe that man will not merely endure, he will prevail . . . because he has a soul, a spirit capable of compassion and sacrifice and endurance."
- To quote Victor Hugo, "If we must suffer, let us suffer nobly."
- To quote the Nike ad campaign, "Just Do It."
- To quote the mass murderer Gary Gilmore's last words before his execution, "Let's do it."
- May we be judged by our actions. As Shakespeare said in *Henry VIII*, "Action is eloquence."
- I don't want to waste my chance to give a toast, so I'll use the words that the famous suffragette Lucy Stone chose for her last words: "Make the world better."
- May we be like mighty oaks, which, after all, are only acorns that held their ground.
- Let us go forth with the resolve of the gladiators who turned to the stands as they entered the arena and said, "Hail, Caesar! We who are about to die salute you."

DEFEAT

- To the School of Hard Knocks—may we graduate from it someday.
- Here's to the men who lose.
  It is the vanquished's praises that I sing,

42

And this is the toast I choose,
"A hard-fought failure is a noble thing!
Here's to the men who lose."

- To our defeat, for, if experience is the best teacher, we are now truly educated.

- Here's to the wisdom of the saying, "If at first you don't succeed, adjust your goals."

- To us—because any direction we go from here is up.

- Let us go forth with the resolve of the gladiators who turned to the stands as they entered the arena and said, "Hail, Caesar! We who are about to die salute you."

- In the words of John F. Kennedy, "Our task is not now to fix blame for the past, but to fix the course for the future."

- Here's to our opponents' victory. May they soon demonstrate that "what goes up, must come down."

- You guys deserved to win. But as Ned Kelly, the Australian outlaw, said as he was being hung, "Such is life."

- You all worked hard on this campaign, and you should congratulate yourselves. To quote Beethoven's last words, "Friends, applaud, the comedy is over."

- To Ruth Gordon, who said, "I think there is one smashing rule: Never face the facts."

- Michel de Montaigne said, "There are some defeats more triumphant than victories." This was one of them. Here's to us.

DENTISTS

- To the man who deals with the tooth, the whole tooth, and nothing but the tooth.

- To the dentist—the person who runs a filling station and is a collector of old magazines.

- Here's to the dentist who got most of his training in the military—as a drill sergeant.

- To the dentist—he makes his living hand to mouth.

DESIRE

- To those who are young, beautiful, and innocent. May we meet soon.

- To darkness—for, as Plutarch said, "When the candles are out all women are fair."

- Drink to the girls and drink to their mothers,
  Drink to their fathers and drink to their brothers;
  Toast their dear healths as long as you're able,
  And dream of their charms while under the table.

- To the wages of sin, which are paying for this occasion.

- Here's to the girl with the big blue eyes,
  Here's to the girl with the milk-white thighs.
  Our eyes have met, our thighs not yet.
  Here's hoping!

  - To the lovely ladies. May they always heed the wise words of Ralph Waldo Emerson, who said, "The only gift is a portion of thyself."

DIET

- To the king of mind over platter.

- Let us eat and drink: for tomorrow we shall die. —Isaiah 22:13

- Eat, drink, and be merry, for tomorrow we diet.

- To the man whose closest contact with a diet is wishful shrinking.

- Here's to us, my good, fat friends,
  To bless the things we eat;
  For it has been full many a year,
  Since we have seen our feet.

DIPLOMATS

- To the diplomat who, as Frederick Sawyer observed, "thinks twice before he says nothing."

- To the diplomat—a person who has learned that you can't bend a nail by hitting it squarely on the head.

- To the diplomat—an ex-politician who has mastered the art of holding his tongue.

- Here's to the diplomat—a person who is held upright by equal pressure from all directions.

- Here's to the diplomat—whose specialty is letting you have her way.

- To the diplomat and diplomacy, which Ambrose Bierce defined as "the patriotic art of lying for one's country."

DIVORCE

- To alimony—the high cost of loving.

- To alimony—man's best proof that you have to pay for your mistakes.

- To alimony—giving comfort to the enemy.

- Here's to your divorce and the messy split
  We're all very happy you got rid of that shit.

- To divorce—the screwing you get for the screwing you got.

- Here's to the divorcée with balls—she believes alimony should be a guaranteed annual wage.

- 'Tis better to have loved and lost
  Than to marry and be bossed.

- To Zsa Zsa Gabor, who said, "I never hated a man enough to give him his diamond back."

- Here's to the high rate of divorce, which Morton Hunt said "reflects not so much the failure of love as the determination of people not to live without it."

DOCTORS

- Physician's toast:
  To mankind we drink: 'tis a pleasant task:
  Heaven bless it and multiply its wealth;
  But it is a little too much to ask
  That we should drink to its health.

- May we always have more occasion for the cook than for the doctor.

- Here's to the vanguards of the medical and legal professions— fond of doctors, little health; fond of lawyers, little wealth.

- In the words of Philip McAllister,
  "Unto our doctors let us drink,
  Who cure our chills and ills,
  No matter what we really think
  About their pills and bills."

- Let's lift our glasses to the doctor—a person to whom we trust our lives and our fortunes.

- Here's to those who heal.

- Here's to a great doctor—the only one I know who thinks a dressing is something you put on a salad.

- Ah, drugs! To quote William Osler, "The desire to take medicine is perhaps the greatest feature which distinguishes man from animals."

DRINK

- In the words of William Morris, "I drink to the days that are."

- Here's to the great artistic genius, Pablo Picasso. His last words were "Drink to me." Who am I to question genius?

- Here's to the best key for unlocking friendship—whis-key.

- Here's to your welcome which was cordial, and your cordial which is welcome.

- Here's to whiskey, scotch, or rye,
Amber, smooth, and clear;
It's not as sweet as a woman's lips,
But a damn sight more sincere.

- To "the corkscrew—a useful key to unlock the storehouse of wit, the treasury of laughter, the front door of fellowship, and the gate of pleasant folly."
—W. E. P. French

- May the beam of the glass never destroy the ray of the mind.

- "For, whether we're right or whether we're wrong,
There's a rose in every thistle

Here's luck—
And a drop to wet your whistle."
—Richard Hovey

- One glass is wholesome, two glasses toothsome, three glasses blithesome, four glasses fulsome, five glasses noisome, six glasses quarrelsome, seven glasses darksome.

- To paraphrase Tom Waits, "May I always have a free bottle in front of me, and never a pre-frontal lobotomy!"

- "Fill the goblet again! For I never before
Felt the glow which now gladdens my heart its core;
Let us drink!—Who would not?—since through life's varied round
In the goblet alone no deception is found."
—Lord Byron

- Any port in a storm. Or any wine, for that matter.

- Let us acknowledge the evils of alcohol and strive to eliminate the wine cellar—one glass at a time.

- Drink rum, drink rum,
Drink rum, by gum with me,
I don't give a damn
For any damn man
That won't take a drink with me.

- Lift 'em high and drain 'em dry
To the guy who says, "My turn to buy!"

- To drinking together, the safest form of sex ever invented.

- Keep your head cool and your feet warm,
And a glass of good whiskey will do you no harm.

- In the immortal words of Ogden Nash, "Candy is dandy, but liquor is quicker."

- To grape expectations.
- Seeing this motley crew gathered here this evening, I'm reminded of a toast made famous by Robert Louis Stevenson:
  "Fifteen men on the dead man's chest—
  Yo-ho-ho and a bottle of rum!
  Drink and the devil had done for the rest—
  Yo-ho-ho and a bottle of rum!"
- Here's to Ms. C. O. Smith who said it best when describing the ideal way to drink one's liquor:
  "How beautiful the water is!
  To me 'tis wondrous sweet—
  For bathing purposes and such;
  But liquor's better neat."
- On land or at sea
  One need not be wary:
  A well-made martini
  Prevents beri-beri.
- May we never be out of spirits.
- Here's to a long life and a merry one,
  A quick death and a happy one,
  A good girl and a pretty one,
  A cold bottle and another one.
- Clink, clink your glasses and drink;
  Why should we trouble borrow?
  Care not for sorrow,
  A fig for the morrow.
  Tonight let's be merry and drink.
- Here's to Miguel de Cervantes who said, "I drink when I have occasion and sometimes when I have no occasion."
- A glass in the hand is worth two on the shelf.
- To drinking: Better to pay the tavernkeeper than the druggist.

- Here's to swearing, lying, stealing and drinking.
  When you swear, swear by your country;
  When you lie, lie for a friend;
  When you steal, steal away from bad company;
  And when you drink, drink with me.

- "Here's lookin' at you, kid!"
  —Rick in *Casablanca*

- Down the hatch!

- Here's mud in your eye.

- Cheers.

- Cheers, cheers, now bring more beers.

- May we always mingle in the friendly bowl,
  The feast of reason and the flow of the soul.

- "What harm in drinking can there be?
  Since punch and life so well agree?"
  —Thomas Blacklock

- Come fill the bowl, each jolly soul!
  Let Bacchus guide this session;
  Join cup to lip with "hip, hip, hip"
  And bury all depression.

- To quote from an old drinking song,
  "Come, landlord, fill the flowing bowl
  Until it does run over.
  For tonight we'll merry be, merry be, merry be,
  Tomorrow we'll get sober."

- In the words of Oliver Goldsmith,
  "Let schoolmasters puzzle their brains
  With grammar and nonsense and learning;
  Good liquor I stoutly maintain,
  Gives genius a better discerning."

- "The man that isn't jolly after drinking
  Is just a driveling idiot, to my thinking."
  —Euripides

- Bottoms up,
  Tops down;
  Wear a smile
  Not a frown.

- May we never want a friend to cheer us, or a bottle to cheer him.

- Here's to the girls of the American shore,
  I love but one, I love no more;
  Since she's not here to drink her part,
  I drink her share with all my heart.

- Up to my lips and over my gums;
  Look out guts, here she comes.

- Here's a health to the king and a lasting peace.
  To faction an end, to wealth increase;
  Come, let's drink it while we have breath,
  For there's no drinking after death.
  And he that will this health deny
  Down among the dead men let him lie!

- "Don't die of love; in heaven above
  Or hell, they'll not endure you;
  Why look so glum when Doctor Rum
  Is waiting for to cure you?"
  —Oliver Herford

EDUCATION

- Let us not forget the words of Oscar Wilde, who said, "Education is an admirable thing, but it is well to remember from time to time that nothing worth knowing can be taught."

- In the words of Oliver Goldsmith,
  "Let schoolmasters puzzle their brains
  With grammar and nonsense and learning;
  Good liquor I stoutly maintain,
  Gives genius a better discerning."

- To the grand endeavor of education. Education pays, they say, but it certainly doesn't pay the educators well!

- To the Dean—who does well despite his faculties.

- To education, which Will and Ariel Durant defined as "the transmission of civilization."

- Cicero said, "To add a library to a house is to give that house a soul." It follows that to give a school a library is to give that school a soul. To our new library—the new soul of our school.

- To our library. As Mrs. Lyndon Baines Johnson said, "Perhaps no place in any community is so democratic as the town library. The only entrance requirement is interest."

ENEMIES

- To our enemies, who have shown us where our faults lie.

- May we treat our friends with kindness and our enemies with generosity.

- To our enemies—we will forgive, but we will never forget.

- May we be happy and our enemies know it.

- In the immortal words of Walt Kelley's Pogo, "We have met the enemy and he is us."

- Here's a health to your enemies' enemies.

- Here's to short shoes and long corns for our enemies.

- May the devil cut the toes off all our foes, that we may know them by their limping.

- May the devil make a ladder of our enemy's backbone while he is picking apples in the garden of hell.

- May a band of gypsies camp in our enemy's belly and train bears to dance on his liver.

- May our foe grow so rotten that goats, skunks, and pigs refuse to be near him.

- May our rival turn into a sparrow and owe his existence to the droppings of a horse.

- May all our enemy's teeth fall out but one—and may that one give him a toothache.

- Here's to you as good as you are,
  And here's to me as bad as I am:
  As good as you are and as bad as I am,
  I'm as good as you are, as bad as I am.

- I've been asked to say something nice about our guest of honor. But I don't see why I should. He's never said anything nice about me.

- In the words of John F. Kennedy, "Forgive your enemies, but don't forget their names."

ENGAGEMENT

- Having seen what receiving a ring has done to our fair friend and the glow it has brought to her face, I finally understand what Edna Ferber meant when she said that jewelry is "a woman's best friend."

- Here's to the happy couple—may you survive your wedding and still be in love.

- In the words of Ralph Waldo Emerson, "Here's to the happy man: All the world loves a lover."

FAMILY

- Here's to your health, and your family's good health. May you live long and prosper.

- To those who know me best and, for some reason, still love me.

- May we be loved by those we love.

- To the sap in our family tree.

FARMING & FARMERS

- Here's to farmers—people who are always out standing in their fields.

- To our fields—may they go to seed.

- To America's farms—they feed the world.

- In the words of E. B. White, "A good farmer is nothing more nor less than a handy man with a sense of humus."

FATHERS

- To the new father—good luck as you enter a "changing" world.

- Here's to my father, the only man that I am afraid of.

- To Dad. May the love and respect we express toward him make up for the worry and care we have visited upon him.

- To my father. If I can become half the man he is, I'll have achieved greatness.

FISHING

- Here's to our fisherman bold;
  Here's to the fish he caught;
  Here's to the one that got away,
  And here's to the ones he bought.

- A fisherman, by the by,
  Will very seldom tell a lie—
  Except when it is needed to
  Describe the fish that left his view.

- As Don Marquis once said, "Here's to fishing—a grand delusion enthusiastically promoted by glorious liars in old clothes."

- Here's to the fish that I may catch;
  So large that even I,
  When talking of it afterward,
  Will never need to lie.

- May the holes in your net be no bigger than your fish.

- Here's to rod and line—may they never part company.

- Here's to our favorite fisherman—may he live to see his stories come true.

- Here's to the one that got away!

- Here's to the noble sport of fishing—a hobby that we are all hooked on!

- Let's lift our glass to the creative fisherman—every time he talks about the one that got away, it grows another foot.

- May good things come to those who bait.

FOOD

- To the alchemy that turns groceries into meals!

- To this meal. In the words of Anthelme Brillat-Savarin, "The creator forcing man to take in food for living invites him through appetite and rewards him with pleasure."

- May we always have more occasion for the cook than for the doctor.

- To quote Mark Twain, "To eat is human, to digest divine."

- To Mom's cooking—may my wife never find out how bad it really was.

- A full belly, a heavy purse, and a light heart.

- I'd rather have dinner while I'm living than a monument when I'm dead, for the dinner will be on my friends, while the monument would be on me.

- To soup—may it be seen and not heard.

- To eat, to drink, and to be merry. —Ecclesiastes 8:15

- To the chef—because, as the famous epicure Anthelme Brillat-Savarin once said, "Discovering a new dish adds more to the happiness of mankind than discovering a new planet."

- As George Bernard Shaw said, "There is no love sincerer than the love of food."

FOURTH OF JULY

- Here's to the memory
  Of the man
  That raised the corn
  That fed the goose
  That bore the quill
  That made the pen
  That wrote the Declaration of Independence.

- In the immortal words of Daniel Webster, "It is my loving sentiment, and by the blessing of God it shall be my dying sentiment—Independence now and Independence forever!"

- To the Fourth of July—for like oyster soup, it cannot be enjoyed without crackers.

- Here's to our country's birthday.

FRATERNITY

- Here's to you and here's to me,
  Wherever we may roam;
  And here's to the health and happiness
  Of the ones who are left at home.

- "The Fraternity of Man—God born and God blessed—its mighty influence for man's betterment can be measured by no human means."
  —Frederick W. Craig

- As we meet on the level, may we part on the square.

FREEDOM

- May we always remember the words of Epictetus, who said, "Only the educated are free."

- My country, great and free!
  Heart of the world, I drink to thee!

- May we be slaves to no party and bigots to no sect.

- To the American eagle—may it never rise in anger, never go to roost in fear.

- To freedom from mobs as well as kings.

- Love, life, and liberty:
  Love pure,
  Life long,
  Liberty boundless.

FRIENDS & FRIENDSHIP

- God gives us our relatives—thank God, we can choose our friends.

- May we never want a friend to cheer us, or a bottle to cheer him.

- When friends with other friends contrive
  To make their glasses clink,
  Then not one sense of all the five
  Is absent from the drink.
  For touch and taste and smell and sight
  Evolve in pleasant round,
  And when the flowing cups unite
  We thrill to sense of sound.
  Folly to look on wine? Oh fie
  On what the teetotalers think . . .
  There's five good reasons why
  Good fellows like to drink.

- Here's to the best key for unlocking friendship—whis-key.

- To quote George Sterling,
  "He who clinks his cup with mine
  Adds a glory to the wine."

- Goodbye, dear ones, and if you need a friend,
  How happy I will be,
  Should you get tired of life's rough way
  Just come and lean on me.
  I'll take you on the smoothest road
  That God to man e'er gave;
  And will go by the longest way
  That takes us to the grave.

- Here's to the man who is wisest and best
  Here's to the man who with judgment is blest,
  Here's to the man who's as smart as can be—
  I drink to the man who agrees with me!

- Here's to one sweetheart, one bottle, and one friend—the
  first beautiful; the second full; and the last ever faithful.

- I'd rather have dinner when I'm living than a monument
  when I'm dead, for the dinner will be on my friends, while
  the monument would be on me.

- A glass is good, and a lass is good,
  And a warm hearth in cold weather.
  The world is good and people are good,
  And we're all good people together.

- Nothing but the best for you. That's why you have us as
  friends.

- A health to you,
  A wealth to you,
  And the best that life can give to you.
  May fortune still be kind to you,
  And happiness be true to you,
  And life be long and good to you,
  Is the toast of all your friends to you.

- Don't walk in front of me,
  I may not follow.
  Don't walk behind me,
  I may not lead.
  Walk beside me,
  And just be my friend.

- Friendship's the wine of life. Let's drink of it and to it.

- Here's to cold nights, warm friends, and a good drink to give them.

- May the friends of our youth be the companions of our old age.

- In the words of Tom Moore, "Pour deep the rosy wine and drink a toast with me. Here's to the three: Thee, Wine, and Camaraderie."

- The world is happy and colorful,
  And life itself is new.
  And I am very grateful for
  The friend I found in you.

- To our best friends, who hear the worst about us but refuse to believe it.

- Forsake not an old friend, for the new is not comparable to him. A new friend is as new wine: when it is old, thou shalt drink it with pleasure. —Ecclesiasticus 9:10

- May the roof above us never fall in, and may we friends gathered below never fall out.

- To goodbyes—that they never be spoken.
  To friendships—may they never be broken.

- Love to one, friendship to a few, and goodwill to all.

- When climbing the hill of prosperity, may we never meet a friend coming down.

- May we have a few real friends rather than a thousand acquaintances.

- May we never have friends who, like shadows, keep close to us in the sunshine, only to desert us on a cloudy day.

- May friendship, like wine, improve as time advances, and may we always have old wine, old friends, and young cares.

- Here's to the friends of tomorrow.

- "May the hinges of friendship never rust, nor the wings of love lose a feather."
  —Dean Ramsay

- Here's to friendship—one soul in two bodies.

- Here's to the tears of friendship. May they crystallize as they fall and be worn as jewels by those we love.

- May we treat our friends with kindness and our enemies with generosity.

- To a true friend—one before whom I can think aloud.

- To a true friend—she knows all about me and loves me just the same.

- A health to our sweethearts, our friends and our wives,
  And may fortune smile on them the rest of their lives.

- To a friend who remembers all the details of our childhood, and has the discretion not to mention them.

- To you, the second most supportive element in my life. I wish I could say you were the most supportive, but at my age, I'm not about to go braless.

- To my friends, who have proved to me the meaning of Cicero's observation that "In friendship we find nothing false or insincere; everything is straightforward and springs from the heart."

61

- To our misspent youth. May our children never be half as rowdy.

- To our friends, who keep city life from being what Henry David Thoreau called it: "Millions of people being lonesome together."

- To perfect friends who were once perfect strangers.

- May you have more and more friends, and need them less and less.

- Here's to our friends,
  As long as we're able
  To lift our glasses
  From the table.

- "Good company, good wine, good welcome. Can make good people."
  —Shakespeare, *Henry VIII*

- One bottle for the four of us—
  Thank God there's no more of us!

- Here's to the true hinges of friendship—
  swearing, lying, stealing, and drinking.
  When you swear, swear by your country;
  When you lie, lie for a pretty woman;
  When you steal, steal away from bad company;
  And when you drink, drink with me.

- Here's to eternity—may we spend it in as good company as this night finds us.

- To our friendship, which, like the wine in this glass, has mellowed and gotten better and better over time.

- To our humorous friend—may you always be healthy, wealthy, and wisecracking.

- Here's to you. You may not be as wise as an owl, but you're always a hoot.

- To all those who tolerated us as we grew up, and all those who tolerate us now.

- "Old wood to burn, old wine to drink, old friends to trust, and old authors to read."
  —Francis Bacon

- Happy are we met, happy have we been,
  Happy may we part, and happy meet again.

- May we ever be able to serve a friend and noble enough to conceal it.

- "Oh! Be thou blest with what heaven can send,
  Long health, long youth, long pleasure—and a friend."
  —Alexander Pope

- "If I do vow a friendship, I'll perform it to the last article."
  —Shakespeare, *Othello*

- Here's to those who love us well,
  Those who don't can go to hell.

- Here's to our absent friends—although out of sight, we recognize them with our glasses.

- To our friends—may their joy be as deep as the ocean, their troubles as light as its foam.

- When we are gathered to carouse, my eloquence fails me, because there's a silly song that runs through my head:
  "Hail, hail, the gang's all here,
  So what the hell do we care?
  What the hell do we care?
  Hail, hail, the gang's all here,
  So what the hell do we care now?"

- May thy life be long and happy,
  Thy cares and sorrows few;
  And the many friends around thee
  Prove faithful, fond and true.

- May our injuries be written in sand and our friendships in marble.

- To my friend, for proving that Ibsen was wrong when he said, "A friend married is a friend lost."

- I salute my long-time friend in the words of La Fontaine, who said, "Friendship is the shadow of the evening which strengthens with the setting sun of life."

- Here's to the friend
  Who listens to my advice,
  Who rejoices in my success,
  Who scorns my enemies,
  Who laughs at my jokes,
  Who ignores my ignorance.

- Wine—to strengthen friendship and light the flame of love.

- "Here's to the fellow who smiles,
  While life rolls on like a song,
  And here's to a chap who can smile,
  When everything goes dead wrong."

GAMBLING

- A little whiskey now and then
  Is relished by the best of men;
  It surely drives away dull care,
  And makes ace high look like two pair.

- Here's to poker. It's like a glass of beer—you draw to fill.

- The hand that rocks the cradle
  Is the hand that rules the earth.
  But the hand that holds four aces—
  Bet on it all you're worth!

- Life consists not in holding good cards, but in playing those you hold well.

- To the race track—where windows clean people.

GENEROSITY

- I propose that we honor our guest with a toast, for our guest has been truly generous, and, as Calvin Coolidge said, "No person was ever honored for what he received. Honor has been the reward for what he gave."

- "I've traveled many a highway
  I've walked for many a mile.
  Here's to the people who made my day
  To the people who waved and smiled."
  —Tom T. Hall

- To our benefactor, whose recent generosity has confirmed what we have long suspected—that he is a remarkable person.

- Lift 'em high and drain 'em dry
  To the guy who says, "My turn to buy!"

- "Drink down all unkindness."
  —Shakespeare, *The Merry Wives of Windsor*

- Here's to riches to the generous and power to the merciful.

- May we strengthen the weak,
  Give light to the blind,
  Clothe the naked,
  And be friends to mankind.

- 'Tis easy to say "Fill 'em"
  When your account's not overdrawn.
  But the man worthwhile,
  Is the man who can smile
  When every damned cent is gone.

GOLF

- To golf—the most frustrating and masochistic sport in the world, which may be why *golf* spelled backward is *flog*.

- Here's to the golfer who just missed a hole-in-one by six strokes.

- To our favorite golfer—may he always be able to find his balls.

- May his investments always be above par, and his game always below.

- May his putter never fail him.

GOOD FORTUNE

- May Dame Fortune ever smile on you, but never her daughter, Miss Fortune.

- May the best of happiness, honor, and fortune keep with you.

- Here's to a full belly, a heavy purse, and a light heart.

- "Lack nothing: be merry."
  —Shakespeare, *1 Henry IV*

- "Heaven give you many, many merry days!"
  —Shakespeare, *The Merry Wives of Windsor*

- May the rocks in your field turn to gold.

- I give you play days, heydays, and pay days!

- May your luck be like the capital of Ireland—"Always Dublin."

- May the frost never afflict your spuds. May the outside leaves of your cabbage always be free from worms. May the crows never pick your haystack and may your donkey always be in foal.

- Here's to blue skies and green lights.

- May your luck ever spread,
  Like jelly on bread.

- To paraphrase a toast once popular among the cowboys, "Here's to luck, and hoping God will take a likin' to us."

- A toast to the three great American birds:
  May you always have an eagle in your pocket,
  A chicken on your table,
  And Wild Turkey in your glass.

- Here's to good luck till we are tired of it.

- May your joys be as deep as the ocean, and your misfortunes as light as its foam.

- May the tide of fortune float us into the harbor of content.

- May bad fortune follow you all your days . . . and never catch up with you.

- May we all have the unspeakable good fortune to win a true heart, and the merit to keep it.

- May you be as lucky as a mosquito in a nudist colony.

- "A flock of blessings light upon thy back."
  —Shakespeare, *Romeo and Juliet*

- Two ins and one out—in health, in wealth, and out of debt.

- May the sunshine of comfort dispel the clouds of despair.

- May the saints protect you,
  And sorrow neglect you,
  And bad luck to the one
  That doesn't respect you.

- May your well never run dry.

- May your fire be as warm as the weather is cold.

- May we never do worse.

- May the clouds in your life be only a background for a lovely sunset.

- May the most you wish for be the least you get.

- Here's to turkey when you're hungry,
  Champagne when you're dry,
  A pretty woman when you need her,
  And heaven when you die.

- In the words of *Star Trek*'s Mr. Spock, "Live long and prosper."

- I wish you all the best. As Shakespeare said in *Timon of Athens*, may "the best of happiness, honor and fortunes keep with you."

- A health to our sweethearts, our friends and our wives,
  And may fortune smile on them the rest of their lives.

GOOD LIFE

- 'Tis hard to tell which is best,
  music, food, drink, or rest.

- A cheerful glass, a pretty lass,
  A friend sincere and true;
  Blooming health, good store of wealth
  Attend on me and you.

- Here's to hell.
  May the stay there

Be as much fun
As the way there.

- To my fellow carousers. As Bertold Brecht once said, "Pleasure-seeking is among the greatest virtues. Wherever it is neglected or maligned, something is rotten."

- Here's to my pipe, a trusty friend indeed,
Filled with that soothing and rest-giving weed,
That fills my soul with peace and joy and laughter—
I'd rather smoke here than in the hereafter.

- May you always distinguish between the weeds and the flowers.

- To the good life. To quote John Henry Voss, he
"Who loves not women, wine, and song,
Remains a fool his whole life long."

- Here's the drinker's last request:
"When I die, don't bury me at all,
Just pickle my bones in alcohol:
A scuttle of booze
At my head and shoes,
And then my bones will surely keep."

GOOD WILL

- Happy are we met,
Happy have we been,
Happy may we part,
And happy meet again.

- May the right person say the right thing
To the right person in the right way,
At the right time, in the right place.

69

- Here's to sunshine and good humor all over the world.

- May the path to hell grow green
  For lack of travelers.

- May you live to learn well, and learn to live well.

- Love to one, friendship to a few, and goodwill to all.

- To goodwill, which Marshall Field called "the one and only asset that competition cannot undersell or destroy."

- May the most you wish for be the least you get.

- Here's to the heart that never wanders and the tongue that never slanders.

- May good nature and good sense always be united.

- May your pleasures be free from the stings of remorse.

GOODBYES

- May you sleep like a log, but not like a sawmill.

- "To all, to each, a fair good night,
  And pleasant dreams and slumbers light."
  —Sir Walter Scott

- Good day, good health, good cheer, good night!

- To goodbyes—that they never be spoken.
  To friendships—may they never be broken.

- May we always part with regret and meet again with pleasure.

- "The pain of parting," said Charles Dickens, "is nothing to the joy of meeting again."

- Goodbye, dear ones, and if you need a friend,
  How happy I will be,

70

Should you get tired of life's rough way
Just come and lean on me.
I'll take you on the smoothest road that God to man e'er
gave;
And will go by the longest way that takes us to the grave.

GRACE

- In the words of the cowboys, "Bless this food and us that
  eats it."

- Heavenly father bless us,
  And keep us all alive;
  There's ten of us for dinner
  And not enough for five.

- For what we are about to receive, may the Lord make us
  truly thankful.

- To this meal. In the words of Anthelme Brillat-Savarin,
  here's to "the creator: Forcing man to take in food for living
  invites him through appetite and rewards him with pleasure."

- Rub-a-dub-dub.
  Thanks for the grub.
  Yeah, God!

- Good bread,
  Good meat,
  Good God,
  Let's eat!

- "Some hae meat, and canna eat,
  And some wad eat that want it;
  But we hae meat, and we can eat,
  And sae the Lord be thankit."
  —Robert Burns

GRADUATION

- To the future, and the leaders of tomorrow.
- Let him be kept from paper, pen and ink.
  That he may cease to write and learn to think.
- A toast to the graduate—in a class by herself.
- I don't want to waste my chance to give you good advice as you go out into the world, so I'll use the words that the famous suffragette Lucy Stone chose for her last words: "Make the world better."
- To all who have just graduated. May you now go on to become educated.
- To our fine educations, may they go to our heads!

GRANDCHILDREN

- To our grandchildren—our revenge on our children!
- To our grandchildren. May we not spoil them *too* much.
- Here's to our grandchildren. May they always carry our name proudly.
- Here's to grandchildren—and the joy of seeing our family enter another generation.
- Here's to grandchildren, gifts from on high.
  (They're God's way of compensating us for growing old.)

GRANDPARENTS

- Here's to grandparents—the cheapest (and best) babysitters on earth.
- To the greatest grandparents—may they live to be great-grandparents.

- Let us raise our glasses
  And then imbibe
  To the splendid couple
  Who founded this tribe.

- To my children's grandparents, the people behind the new G.I. plan—Generous In-laws!

GRATITUDE

- I feel like a loaf of bread. Wherever I go they toast me.

- May we be content with our lot, which, when you think about it, is quite a lot.

- After everything that has happened, I can only quote the last words of Czar Alexander I of Russia: "What a beautiful day."

- To all who applauded us—as the cow said to the farmer, "Thank you for a warm hand on a cold morning."

- Thanks for your cordial, which was welcome; and for your welcome, which was cordial.

GUESTS

- In the truly immortal words of Bram Stoker's Count Dracula, "Welcome to my house. Come freely. Go safely. And leave something of the happiness you bring!"

- Here's a toast to all who are here,
  No matter where you're from;
  May the best day you have seen
  Be worse than your worst to come.

- To our guests. Our house is ever at your service.

- Here's to our guest—
  Don't let him rest,
  But keep his elbow bending.
  'Tis time to drink—
  Full time to think
  Tomorrow—when you're mending.

- In the words of Myrtle Reed, "May our house always be too small to hold all our friends."

- "The ornament of a house is the guests who frequent it."
  —Ralph Waldo Emerson

- By the bread and salt, by the water and wine,
  You are welcome, friends, at this table of mine.

- "Come in the evening, or come in the morning—
  Come when you're looked for, or come without warning;
  A thousand welcomes you'll find here before you,
  The oftener you come here the more I'll adore you."
  —Thomas O. Davis

- "Good company, good wine, good welcome. Can make good people."
  —Shakespeare, *Henry VIII*

- As Thomas Lipton once said, "Here's to all of us."

- In the words of Rudyard Kipling, "Here's to us that are here, to you that are there, and the rest of us everywhere."

- Love to one, friendship to many, and goodwill to all.

- Here's a health to thee and thine
  From the hearts of me and mine;
  And when thee and thine
  Come to see me and mine,
  May me and mine make thee and thine
  As welcome as thee and thine
  Have ever made me and mine.

74

HAPPINESS

- May every day be happier than the last.

- The best of happiness, honor, and fortunes keep with you.

- May we look forward with happiness, and backward without regret.

- Let us not flounder in following the founders' direction toward life, liberty and, most of all, the pursuit of happiness.

- May your joys be as deep as the ocean, and your misfortunes as light as its foam.

- May our pleasures be free from the stings of remorse.

- "I drink to the general joy of the whole table."
  —Shakespeare, *Macbeth*

- May the frowns of misfortune never rob innocence of its joy.

- Here's to happiness. In the words of John Wolcott,
  "Care to our coffin adds a nail, no doubt,
  And every grin, so merry, draws one out."

- To the three H's: health, honor, and happiness.
  Health to the world,
  Honor to those who seek for it,
  Happiness in our homes.

- May we be happy and our enemies know it.

- To quote John Dryden, here's to a "merry, dancing, drinking, laughing, quaffing, and unthinking time."

- A full belly, a heavy purse, and a light heart.

- I wish you all the best. As Shakespeare said in *Timon of Athens*, may "the best of happiness, honor and fortunes keep with you."

HEALTH

- "We drink one another's healths and spoil our own."
—Jerome K. Jerome

- As Shakespeare said in *The Merry Wives of Windsor*, let us "drink down all unkindness."

- Here's health to those I love, and wealth to those who love me.

- Health to our sweethearts, our friends and our wives;
And may fortune smile on them the rest of their lives.

- Here's to your health, and your family's good health, and may you live long and prosper.

- To the three H's: health, honor, and happiness.
Health to the world,
Honor to those who seek for it,
Happiness in our homes.

- Here's to your health—a long life and an easy death to you.

- Here's to your health! You make age curious, time furious, and all of us envious.

- Here's to health, peace, and prosperity—may the flower of love never be nipped by the frost of disappointment, nor the shadow of grief fall upon a member of this circle.

- Here's to your health. May God bring you luck, and may your journey be smooth and happy.

- To your health. May we drink one together in ten years' time and a few in between.

- A good wife and health
Are a man's best wealth.

- Here's to health to my soul and health to my heart;
Where this is going, there's gone many a quart.

Through my teeth and round my gums;
Look out, belly, here it comes.

- May the Lord love us but not call us too soon.

- To you, and yours, and theirs, and mine,
  I pledge with you, their health in wine.

- Here's a health to thee and thine
  From the hearts of me and mine;
  And when thee and thine
  Come to see me and mine,
  May me and mine make thee and thine
  As welcome as thee and thine
  Have ever made me and mine.

- Here's health to all who need it.

- Health to our sweethearts, our friends and our wives,
  And may fortune smile on them the rest of their lives.

- I drink to your health when I'm with you,
  I drink to your health when I'm alone,
  I drink to your health so often
  I'm beginning to worry about my own.

- To your very good health. May you live to be as old as your jokes.

HOME

- May your fire be as warm as the weather is cold.

- May your well never run dry.

- To home—where we always find warm words on a cold day.

- To home—the place where we receive the best treatment and which we appreciate the least.

- Here's to home, where a world of strife is shut out and a world of love is shut in.

- God bless this mess.

- God bless our mortgaged home.

- Here's to our town—a place where people spend money they haven't earned to buy things they don't need to impress people they don't like.

- "The ornament of a house is the guests who frequent it." —Ralph Waldo Emerson

- To the pleasures of home: a good book, a bright light, and an easy chair.

- To home—the place where you're treated best and grumble most.

- To home—the father's kingdom; the child's paradise; the mother's world.

- In the words of the old song,
  "Oh my!
  I'm too young to die,
  I wanna go home!"

- To our friendly, cozy little burg, where no one can sing "Nobody knows the trouble I've seen."

HOSTS & HOSTESSES

- To our host, a most excellent man; for is not a man fairly judged by the company he keeps?

- Here's to your welcome which was cordial, and your cordial which is welcome.

- Here's to the hostess and host—
  Jolly good health in this toast.
  May your journey be good
  On the road that you choose,
  Though it be fast or slow,
  And joy attend you all the way
  Whichever road you go.

- To our hostess. She's a gem. We love her, God bless her.
  And the devil take her husband.

- To our host who gives us what Henry Sambrooke Leigh described as "the rapturous, wild, and ineffable pleasure of drinking at somebody else's expense."

- What's a table richly spread
  Without this woman at its head?

- Here's a toast to our host from all of us;
  May he soon be the guest of each of us.

- Here's to our hostess, considerate and sweet;
  Her wit is endless, but when do we eat?

- To the sun that warmed the vineyard,
  To the juice that turned to wine,
  To the host that cracked the bottle,
  And made it yours and mine.

- To our friend, who is neither an optimist who sees a glass as half full, nor a pessimist who sees a glass as half empty; but a host, who sees it as a glass that needs topping off.

- Let us raise our glasses high and thank our host for the pleasure of being his company.

- To our host, who has the ability to make us all feel at home, even though that's where he wishes we were.

- To our hostess with the most-ess.

- Here's a toast to the host who carved the roast;
  And a toast to the hostess—may she never roast us.

- Here's to the hostess and here's to the host,
  As we raise up our glasses and offer this toast;
  Thank you for this lovely meal,
  Thank you for these friends so real,
  Thank you for the way we feel.
  We think you're just the most.

- To our host: happiness, health and prosperity.

- Here's to the bride
  And here's to the groom
  And to the bride's father
  Who'll pay for this room.

HUMOR

- To thrift—and our ancestors who practiced it so that we don't have to.

- Though life is now pleasant and sweet to the sense
  We'll be damnably moldy a hundred years hence.

- "Remember the poor—it costs nothing."
  —Josh Billings

- "Life is a jest, and all things show it—
  I thought so once, but now I know it."
  —John Gay

- To procrastination, which has saved us from innumerable mistakes.

- Here's to the bee—the busy soul;
  He has no time for birth control.

That's why it is in times like these,
We have so many sons of bees!

- To the bore—may he give us a few brilliant flashes of silence.

- Here's to the bore—the only one who can monopolize and monotonize a conversation at the same time.

- We know it's true that we're wicked,
  That our criminal laws are lax;
  But here's to punishment for the man
  Who invented our income tax.

- To the laughter which we all have shared, because, as Victor Borge said, "Laughter is the shortest distance between two people."

- To our humorous friend—may you always be healthy, wealthy and wisecracking.

- Here's to you. You may not be as wise as an owl, but you're always a hoot.

- Here's to the man who is wisest and best
  Here's to the man who with judgment is blest,
  Here's to the man who's as smart as can be—
  I drink to the man who agrees with me!

- Now, let us grasp our glasses and, while our arms are raised to the sky, let us be thankful to the inventor of underarm deodorant.

- So, now, in tribute to our host and this momentous occasion, please raise your glasses . . . of cheap wine.

- Laugh and the world laughs with you;
  Weep, and it laughs at you anyway.

- To your very good health. May you live to be as old as your jokes.

- Here's to a man after my own heart. And after my house and my wife . . .

- Wise, kind, gentle, generous, sexy . . . but enough about me. Here's to you.

- To a fine man who remembers where he came from. Of course, that's about all he remembers.

- Here's to the brilliant, warm, handsome . . . company that you keep.

- Nothing but the best for our hostess. That's why she has us as friends.

- To the voice we speak to every day—to your answering machine.

- To a man too brilliant to ever be popular. Misery loves company.

- To our host who is living proof that God has a sense of humor.

- May every man be what he thinks himself to be.

- May we never be out of spirits.

- Here's to our boss, when he tells you not to worry—start worrying.

- To the model husband—any other woman's.

- All the best to you, from one who remembers when you were an immature brat . . . last week.

- I raise my glass to say:
  It's your birthday, that's true;
  And to celebrate the fact
  That I'm younger than you.

- Here's to you—you labored so hard for so many years to furnish us with a splendidly bad example.
- May your coffee and slanders against you be ever alike—without grounds.

HUSBANDS & WIVES

Husbands

- To the first man who could win both my heart and my mother's approval.
- Here's to a man who loves his wife, and loves his wife alone. For many a man loves another man's wife, when he ought to be loving his own.
- To the model husband—any other woman's.
- Here's to the man who is wisest and best,
  Here's to the man with judgment is blest.
  Here's to the man who's as smart as can be—
  I mean the man who agrees with me.
- To our sweethearts and husbands. May they never meet.
- Here's to the husband who can bravely say,
  "I have loved her, all my life—
  Since I took her hand on the wedding day
  I have only loved my wife."
- A good husband and health
  Are a woman's best wealth.

Wives

- To my wife—my bride and joy.
- A good wife and health
  Are a man's best wealth.

- Here's to the wife I love,
  And here's to the wife who loves me,
  And here's to all those who love her whom I love
  And all those who love her who love me.

- To my wife and our anniversary, which I forgot once, but will never forget again.

- Here's to our wives—may they be as blissfully trustful as we are trustfully blissful.

- A health to our sweethearts, our friends and our wives,
  And may fortune smile on them the rest of their lives.

- Here's to our sweethearts and our wives;
  May our sweethearts soon become our wives,
  And our wives ever remain our sweethearts.

- Here's to our wives!
  They keep our hives
  In little bees and honey;
  They darn our socks,
  They soothe life's shocks,
  And don't they spend the money!

- Here's to the pretty woman
  I fought to marry at all cost.
  The struggle was well worth it,
  'Cause without her I'd be lost.

- To my wife:
  Here's to the prettiest, here's to the wittiest,
  Here's to the truest of all who are true,
  Here's to the nearest one, here's to the sweetest one,
  Here's to them, all in one—here's to you.

- To our wives and sweethearts. May they never meet!

- A health to our widows. If they ever marry again, may they do as well!

Husbands & Wives

- To the person who makes my days a delight. And if you think I'm going to talk in public about our nights, you're crazy.

- To my spouse, who has also been my best adviser.

- Here's to the husband—
  And here's to the wife;
  May they remain lovers for life.

IMAGINATION

- To imagination. As Albert Einstein said, "Imagination is more important than knowledge."

- To imagination and all it does for us. As Shakespeare said in *Richard III*, "True hope is swift and flies with swallow's wings, kings it makes gods, and meaner creatures, kings."

- Here's to imagination. R. Buckminster Fuller said it best: "Dare to be naive."

- As Jules de Gaultier said, "In the war against reality man has one weapon—imagination."

INFIDELITY

- Here's to the pictures on my desk. May they never meet.

- Here's to the man who loves his wife,
  And loves his wife alone;
  For many a man loves another man's wife,
  When he ought to be loving his own.

- To our wives and sweethearts—may they never meet!
- May our marriages never interfere with our love lives.
- May your wedding ring never act as a tourniquet and cut down on your circulation.
- May you die at age ninety shot by the jealous husband of a teenager.
- May we kiss those we please, and please those we kiss.
- Here's to the bachelor who's decided to take a wife—but hasn't yet decided whose.

INTERNATIONAL

Austrian, German

- *Prosit.* (To your health.)

French

- *Plus je bois, mieux je chante.* (The more I drink, the better I sing.)
- *A vôtre santé.* (To your health.)

Irish

- *Slainte* (pronounced *slawn*-cheh). (Your health.)
- Here's to the land of the shamrock so green,
  Here's to each lad and his darling colleen,
  Here's to the ones we love dearest and most,
  And may God Bless old Ireland!—that's an Irishman's toast.

Italian

- *Salute.* (Your health.)

Japanese

- *Kan pai*. (Bottoms up.)

Jewish

- *L'chayim*. (To life.)
- *Mazel tov*. (Congratulations.)

Latin

- *Dum vivimus vivamus*. (Let us live while we live.)
- *Dilige amicos*. (Love your friends.)
- *Propino tibi*. (I drink to you.)

PigLatin

- Eers-chay. (Cheers.)

Russian

- *Na zdorovia*. (To your health.)

Scandinavian

- *Skoal*. (Your health.)

Spanish

- *Salud*. (Your health.)

IRREVERENCE

- Here's to the bride
  And here's to the groom
  And to the bride's father
  Who'll pay for this room.

- Here's to your wedding and many of them.

- Here's to a clear conscience—or a poor memory.

- Here's to conscience. May it wake to hear us toast it and then go to sleep again.

- To the cocktail party where olives are speared and friends stabbed.

- Heavenly father bless us,
  And keep us all alive;
  There's ten of us for dinner
  And not enough for five.

- Here's to our hostess, considerate and sweet;
  Her wit is endless, but when do we eat?

- I feel just like a loaf of bread. Wherever I go—they toast me.

- Here's looking at you, though heaven knows it's an effort.

- Here's mud in your eyes—while I look over your beautiful sweetheart.

- Good bread,
  good meat,

good God,
let's eat.

- Rub-a-dub-dub,
Thanks for the grub.
Yeah, God!

- The God Cheer:
Big G!
Little o-d
Go with the grace of God—
Rah!

- Here's to hell!
May the stay there
Be as much fun as the way there!

- To the honeymoon, so called because it is so sweet compared with the bitter months that follow.

- The Biker's Toast
"Thank you, God, for this daily bread,
LSD and the Grateful Dead.
For all the things we love and like
And thank you God, for my bike."

- To the lie—an abomination unto the Lord, and a very present help in time of trouble.

- In the words of Mark Twain, "May every liar be blessed with a good memory."

- Here's to love. It begins with a fever and ends with a yawn.

- Love makes time pass—
Time makes love pass.

KISS

- Here's some food for thought,
  I heard it at a recent ball,
  'Tis better to be kissed and caught
  Than never to be kissed at all.

- May we kiss those we please, and please those we kiss.

- They say there're microbes in a kiss,
  This rumor is most rife.
  Come lady dear, and make of me
  An invalid for life.

- Here's to the lasses we've loved, my lad,
  Here's to the lips we've pressed;
  For of kisses and lasses
  Like liquor in glasses,
  The last is always the best.

- Here's to four sweet lips, two pure souls, and one undying
  affection—love's perfect ingredients for a kiss.

- "Drink to me only with thine eyes,
  And I will pledge with mine;
  Or leave a kiss within the cup,
  And I'll not look for wine."
  —Ben Jonson

LAW & LAWYERS

- Here's to the law—a bad compromise beats a good lawsuit.

- "And do as adversaries in law—
  Strive mightily, but eat and drink as friends."
  —Shakespeare, *The Taming of the Shrew*

- "A bumper of good liquor
  Will end a contest quicker
  Than justice, judge or vicar;
  So fill a cheerful glass,
  and let good humor pass."
  —Richard Brinsley Sheridan

- In the words of Charles Macklin, to "the glorious uncertainty of the law."

- In Shakespeare's immortal words from *Henry VI*, "The first thing we do, let's kill all the lawyers."

- To the lawyer who knows it's often better to know the judge than it is to know the law.

- Here's to the vanguards of the medical and legal professions. As they say,
  Fond of doctors, little health;
  Fond of lawyers, little wealth.

- Here's a toast to a man of great trials and many convictions.

- Here's to the lawyer—a bright gentleman, who rescues your estate from your enemies, and keeps it himself.

- To lawyers. In the words of Joseph H. Choate, "You cannot live without the lawyers, and certainly you cannot die without them."

- Here's to the advice my lawyer gave me:
  Say it with flowers
  Say it with eats,
  Say it with kisses,
  Say it with sweets,
  Say it with jewelry,
  Say it with drink,
  But always be careful
  Not to say it with ink.

LIFE

- To life—a fatal, hereditary disease.

- Life consists not in holding good cards, but in playing those you hold well.

- "May you live all the days of your life."
  —Jonathan Swift

- Let us wipe out the past, trust in the future, and rejoice in the glorious Now.

- "Life is a jest, and all things show it—
  I thought so once, but now I know it."
  —John Gay

- Every day should be passed as though it were our last.

- Let us eat and drink; for tomorrow we shall die. —Isaiah 22:13

- Here's to love, life, and liberty:
  Love pure,
  Life long,
  Liberty boundless.

- To life. The first half is ruined by our parents and the second half by our children.

LONG LIFE

- May the Lord love us but not call us too soon.

- May you enter heaven late.

- Long life to you and may you die in your bed.

- May you live to be a hundred—and decide the rest for yourself.

- May you die in bed at age ninety-five shot by the jealous husband of a teenage wife.

- Till a hundred and twenty.

LOVE

- Let's drink to love, which is nothing—unless it's divided by two.

- While there's life on the lip,
  While there's warmth in the wine,
  One deep health I'll pledge,
  And that health shall be thine.

- May we all have the unspeakable good fortune to win a true heart, and the merit to keep it.

- To love, or as Martin Tupper once said, "Love—what a volume in a word, an ocean in a tear!"

- "A mighty pain to love it is,
  And 'tis a pain that pain to miss;
  But, of all pains, the greatest pain,
  Is to love, but love in vain."
  —Abraham Cowley

- "Don't die of love; in heaven above
  Or hell, they'll not endure you;
  Why look so glum when Doctor Rum
  Is waiting for to cure you?"
  —Oliver Herford

- May those now love
  Who never loved before;
  May those who've loved
  Now love the more.

- Here's to love: A little sighing, a little crying, a little dying—and a touch of white lying.

- Wine, to strengthen friendship and light the flame of love.

- To Cupid, whom George Farquhar called the "blind gunner."

- Here's to love, a thing so divine,
  Description makes it but the less.
  'Tis what we feel, but cannot define,
  'Tis what we know but cannot express.

- Here's to lovers everywhere—the have-beens, the are-nows, and the may-bes.

- In the words of James Keene, "Here's to those who love us well—those who don't may go to hell."

- Here's to the love that I hold for thee;
  May it day by day grow stronger:
  May it last as long as your love for me—
  And not a second longer!

- Here's to love, life, and liberty.
  Love pure,
  Life long,
  Liberty boundless.

- A thousand welcomes you will find here before you,
  And the oftener you come here the more I'll adore you.

- Because I love you truly,
  Because you love me, too,
  My very greatest happiness
  Is sharing life with you.

- Here's to one and only one,
  And may that one be he
  Who loves but one and only one,
  And may that one be me.

- Here's to the prettiest, here's to the wittiest,
  Here's to the truest of all who are true,
  Here's to the neatest one, here's to the sweetest one,
  Here's to them all wrapped in one—here's to you.

- Here's to this water,
  Wishing it were wine,
  Here's to you, my darling,
  Wishing you were mine.

- Here's to you who halves my sorrows and doubles my joys.

- I love you more than yesterday, less than tomorrow.

- May we love as long as we live, and live as long as we love.

- In the words of Sir Walter Scott,
  "To every lovely lady bright,
  I wish a gallant faithful knight;
  To every faithful lover, too,
  I wish a trusting lady true."

- To the land we love, and the love we land.

- Love to one, friendship to a few, and goodwill to all.

- Here's to love—the disease that begins with a fever and ends with a pain.

- May we have those in our arms whom we love in our hearts.

- To the wings of love—
  May they never lose a feather,
  But soar up to the sky above,
  And last and last forever.

- "A book of verses underneath the bough,
  A jug of wine, a loaf of bread, and thou."
  —Omar Khayyam

- To the life we love with those we love.

- "Drink to me only with thine eyes,
  And I will pledge with mine;
  Or leave a kiss within the cup,
  And I'll not look for wine."
  —Ben Jonson

- Here's to my sweetheart's eyes,
  Those homes of emotion.
  Oh, how they make me think.
  I like them sad.
  I prefer them glad.
  But I love them when they wink.

- I have known many,
  Liked a few,
  Loved one—
  Here's to you.

- Here's to love, the only fire against which there is no insurance.

- Here's to the woman who loves me
  And here's to the many who don't;
  Here's to the girl who accepts me,
  And here's to the many who won't.

- To love. Dorothy Parker described it as the "quicksilver in the hand. Leave the fingers open and it stays in the palm; clutch it and it darts away."

- May we be loved by those we love.

- Say it with flowers,
  Say it with eats,
  Say it with kisses,
  Say it with sweets,
  Say it with jewelry,

Say it with drink,
But always be careful
Not to say it with ink.

- Thou hast no faults, or no faults I can spy;
  Thou art all beauty, or all blindness I.

- To quote Elbert Hubbard, "The love you give away is the only love you keep."

- May we kiss those we please, and please those we kiss.

- "'Tis better to have loved and lost,
  Than never to have loved at all."
  —Alfred, Lord Tennyson

- 'Tis better to have loved and lost,
  Than to marry and be bossed.

- To moderation in all things—except in love.

- Here's to the red and sparkling wine,
  I'll be your sweetheart, if you'll be mine,
  I'll be constant, I'll be true,
  I'll leave my happy home for you.

- The world is filled with flowers,
  The flowers filled with dew,
  The dew is filled with love
  For you, and you, and you.

- Here's to those who'd love us
  If only we cared.
  Here's to those we'd love
  If only we dared.

- To the life we love with those we love.

LUSHES

- Here's to a real drinker—he doesn't just drown his problems, he irrigates them.

- Drink to me only with thine eyes,
  And I will pledge with mine;
  For I would have to pawn my watch
  If you should drink more wine.

- On this occasion, it's only appropriate to recite a few words
  of an old drinking song:
  "I was drunk last night,
  Drunk the night before;
  Going to get drunk tonight
  Till I fall down on the floor.
  'Cause when I'm drunk
  I'm as happy as can be:
  For I am a member
  Of the souse family."

- If I drink too much of your liquor,
  And should be foolish enough to get tight,
  Would you be a perfect gentleman,
  And see that I get home all right?

- Here's to man who is, in the words of Voltaire "the only
  animal that laughs, drinks when he is not thirsty, and makes
  love at all seasons of the year."

- Here's to the serpent in the glass—
  There's always one in mine;
  And when he gets into my legs
  I travel serpentine.

- Better to pay the tavernkeeper than the druggist.

- Come, friends, come let us drink again,
  This liquid from the nectar vine,
  For water makes you dumb and stupid,
  Learn this from the fishes—
  They cannot sing, nor laugh, nor drink
  This beaker full of sparkling wine.

- In the words of Artemus Ward, "Drink with impunity—or anyone who happens to invite you."

- He who goes to bed, and goes to bed sober,
Falls as the leaves do, and dies in October;
But he who goes to bed, and does so mellow,
Lives as he ought to, and dies a good fellow.

- To moderation. I agree with François Rabelais, who said, "I drink no more than a sponge."

- I drink to your health when I'm with you,
I drink to your health when I'm alone,
I drink to your health so often
I'm beginning to worry about my own.

- Here's to Miguel de Cervantes, who said, "I drink when I have occasion and sometimes when I have no occasion."

- Here's to alcohol. In the immortal words of William Shakespeare from *Richard III*, "Kings it makes gods, and meaner creatures, kings."

- "O water!" said W. E. P. French,
"Pure, free of pollution.
I vainly wished that I dared trust it.
But I've an iron constitution,
And much I fear that water'd rust it."

- Here's to W. Knox Haynes, who said,
"One drink is plenty;
Two drinks too many,
And three not half enough."

- They that drink deepest live longest.

- "'Tis a pity," said Lord Byron,
"Wine should be so deleterious,
For tea and coffee leave us much more serious."

- Too much is never enough.

MARRIAGE

- Here's to matrimony, the high sea for which no compass has yet been invented.

- To marriage—the happy estate which, as Sydney Smith observed, "resembles a pairs of shears; so joined that they cannot be separated; often moving in opposite directions, yet always punishing anyone who comes between them."

- May all single men get married,
  and all married men be happy.

- Here's to the man who loves his wife,
  And loves his wife alone—
  For many a man loves another man's wife
  When he might be loving his own.

- To the wonderful institution called marriage. It's one of the few relationships where, as Elbert Hubbard said, "Man's boldness and woman's caution make an excellent business arrangement."

- To marriage—an institution very much like a tourniquet because it stops your circulation.

- To marriage—the last decision a man is allowed to make.

- To a happy marriage, or in the words of André Maurois, "To a long conversation that always seems too short."

- To a second marriage, which Samuel Johnson described as "the triumph of hope over experience."

- Here's to the married woman—a mistress of arts, who robs a man of his bachelor's degree and forces him by lectures to study philosophy.

- May their joys be as deep as the ocean
  And their misfortunes as light as the foam.

100

- May you grow old on one pillow.

- May you have many children; and may they grow as mature in taste, and as healthy in color, and as sought after as the contents of this glass.

- May your love be as endless as your wedding rings.

- Parents' toast: "It is written: When children find true love, parents find true joy." Here's to your joy and ours, from this day forward.

- Needles and pins, needles and pins
  When a man marries his troubles begin.

MEN

- Here's to the men, God bless them!
  Worst of my sins, I confess them,
  Is loving them all, be they great or small,
  So here's to the boys! God bless them!

- May all single men get married, and all married men be happy.

- Here's to the man who is wisest and best,
  Here's to the man who with judgment is blest.
  Here's to the man who's as smart as can be—
  I mean the man who agrees with me.

- To men—who divide our time, double our cares, and triple our troubles.

- To men—creatures who buy playoff tickets months in advance and wait until Christmas Eve to buy presents.

- To the two things that delight a young girl's heart—fresh flowers and fresh men.

- Here's to the men of all classes
  Who through lasses and glasses
  Will make themselves asses!

- "Man is the only animal who laughs, drinks when he is not thirsty, and makes love at all seasons of the year."
  —Voltaire

- Women's faults are many,
  Men have only two—
  Everything they say,
  And everything they do.

- Here's to the fellow who smiles,
  While life rolls on like a song,
  But here's to the chap who can smile,
  When everything goes dead wrong.

- Here's to the gentlemen—first in our hearts and first in our pocketbooks.

- Women, beware of men! To quote an old song ("Frankie and Johnny"),
  "This story has no moral,
  This story has no end,
  This story only goes to show
  That there ain't no good in men.
  They'll do you wrong just as sure's you're born."

MILITARY

Army

- Here's to the soldier who fights and loves—may he never lack for either.

- In the words of Colonel Blacker, "Put your trust in God, boys, and keep your powder dry."

- "The girl and boy are bound by a kiss,
  But there's never a bond, old friend like this:
  We have drunk from the same canteen."
  —General Charles G. Halpine

- To our women, our horses, and the men who ride them.

- Here's to the soldier and his arms,
  Fall in, men, fall in;
  Here's to women and their arms,
  Fall in, men, fall in.

Marines

- Here's health to you and to our corps,
  Which we are proud to serve:
  In many a strife we have fought for life
  And never lost our nerve.
  If the army and the navy
  Ever look on heaven's scenes,
  They will find the streets are guarded
  By the United States Marines.

- I give you muscles of steel, nerves of iron, tongues of silver, hearts of gold, necks of leather—the marines.

- As Sir Walter Scott said, "Tell that to the marines."

Navy

- To the wisdom of sailors. As Sir Walter Scott said, "Tell that to the marines—the sailors won't believe it."

- To our sailors—long may they ride the waves.

- To our navy—may it ever float.

103

- Here's to the ships of our navy,
  And the ladies of our land;
  May the first be ever well rigged,
  And the latter ever well manned.

- A stout ship, a clear sea, and a far-off coast in stormy weather.

- Here's to the navy—true hearts and sound bottoms.

- Here's to grog, grub, and glory.

- To the sailor—the only person I know who gets seasick taking a bath.

Miscellaneous

- Here's to American valor,
  May no war require it, but may it ever be ready for every foe.

- In the words of Minna Thomas Antrim, "Here's to Uncle Sam's fighters—models of all that's brave, terrors to all who are unfair."

- Here's to the army and navy,
  And the battles they have won,
  Here's to America's colors—
  The colors that never run.

- Here's to the land we love and the love we land.

MISTAKES

- May our faults be written on the seashore, and every good action prove a wave to wash them out.

- May we never do worse.

- May we never be blind to our own mistakes.

- To procrastination, which has saved 'us from innumerable mistakes.

MODERATION & ABSTINENCE

Pro

- May the bloom of the face never extend to the nose.

- One swallow doesn't make a summer, but it breaks a New Year's resolution.

- A toast to any gentleman
  So shrewd and diplomatic
  Who never—though he's in his cups—
  Decides he's operatic.

- To abundance, abstinence, and annihilation.
  Abundance to the poor,
  Abstinence to the intemperate,
  Annihilation to the wicked.

- May our imagination never run away with our judgment.

- May the beam of the glass never destroy the ray of the mind.

- See our glorious banner waving,
  Hear the bugle call;
  Rally comrades to the standard
  Down with alcohol.

- To mirth, music, and moderation.
  Mirth at every board,
  Music in all instruments,
  Moderation in our desires.

- Here's to the fall of Bacchus—he's drowned more men than Neptune.

- If you drink like a fish, drink what a fish drinks.

- "We drink one another's healths and spoil our own."
  —Jerome K. Jerome

- May we never be influenced by jealousy nor governed by interest.

- To moderation in all things—except in love.

- May we fly from the temptation we cannot resist.

- First the man takes a drink;
  Then the drink takes a drink,
  Then the drink takes the man.

- Here's to wine, wit, and wisdom.
  Wine enough to sharpen wit,
  Wit enough to give zest to wine,
  Wisdom enough to "shut down" at the right time.

- To wine—may those who use it never abuse it.

- To the best throw of the dice—throwing them away!

- To water—we never want cash to buy it, we are never ashamed to ask for it, and we never blush to drink it.

- Here's to a temperance supper
  With water in glasses tall,
  And coffee and tea to end with—
  And good health to one and all.

- Here's to abstinence—may it continue to reduce the number of men who think they can sing.

- Our drink shall be water, bright, sparkling with glee,
  The gift of our God, and the drink of the free.

Con

- Here's to a temperance supper,
  With water in glasses tall,
  And coffee and tea to end with—
  And me not there at all.

- God, in his goodness, sent the grapes
  To cheer both great and small;
  Little fools will drink too much,
  And great fools none at all.

- "Not drunk is he who from the floor
  Can rise again and drink some more;
  But drunk is he who prostrate lies,
  And who can neither drink nor rise."
  —Eugene Field

- "'Tis a pity wine should be so deleterious,
  For tea and coffee leave us much more serious."
  —Lord Byron

- Here's to abstinence—as long as it's practiced in moderation.

- To our sense of moderation—may we relocate it tomorrow!

MONEY

- To the good old days, when big spenders used their own money!

- To prosperity, for, as John Ray said, "Money cures melancholy."

- May the weight of our taxes never bend the back of our credit.

- To the almighty dollar, without which we would have no cents.

- To money—the finest linguist in the world.

- Here's to the mints—the only places that make money without advertising.

- To the spirit of charity. As Clint W. Murchison said, "Money is like manure. If you spread it around, it does a lot of good, but if you pile it up in one place, it stinks like hell."

MOTHERS

- To the mother who bore me,
  There's no one more bold,
  She's dearer by far
  Than all of earth's gold.

- To our mothers, God bless them every one.
  May the eyes of the Fathers and the love of the Sons
  Watch over and protect them—keep them holy and pure,
  With life to sustain and health to endure.

- We have toasted our sweethearts,
  Our friends and our wives,
  We have toasted each other
  Wishing all merry lives;
  Don't frown when I tell you
  This toast beats all others,
  But drink one more toast, boys—
  A toast to—our mothers.

- Here's to the happiest hours of my life—
  Spent in the arms of another man's wife—
  My mother!

- It's not the woman with ebon locks,
  Nor the one with head of brown,

Nor the lady fair with the golden hair,
Nor the one with the copper crown.
But the woman I love the best of all,
And the one I toast tonight,
With her smiling face and easy grace,
Wears a mane of shimmering white—
My mother.

- To our father's sweethearts—our mothers.

- To our mothers and all that they have meant to us. They are the proof of the Jewish proverb that "God could not be everywhere, so he made mothers."

MOTHERS-IN-LAW

- Here's to my mother-in-law, who let me take her baby from her—without too much of a fight.

- To my mother-in-law, who has finally stopped regarding me as the outlaw.

- Here's to my mother-in-law, because as Brooks Hays once said, "Behind every successful man stands a proud wife and a surprised mother-in-law."

MUSIC

- Here's to music, which Henry Wadsworth Longfellow called "the universal language of mankind."

- To the soothing influence of music. As William Congreve said, "Music hath charms to soothe the savage breast."

- To music, which John Erskine called "the only language in which you cannot say a mean or sarcastic thing."

- To music. As Friedrich Nietzsche said, "Without music, life would be a mistake."

- To mirth, music, and moderation.
  Mirth at every board,
  Music in all instruments,
  Moderation in our desires.

- Let's lift our glass to the conductor—a person who rarely composes himself.

NEW YEAR

- Welcome be ye that are here,
  Welcome all, and make good cheer,
  Welcome all, another year.

- Another year is dawning. Let it be true
  For better or for worse, another year with you.

- May all your troubles during the coming year be as short as your New Year's resolutions.

- Here's to a bright New Year
  And a fond farewell to the old;
  Here's to the things that are yet to come
  And to the memories that we hold.

- One swallow doesn't make a summer, but it breaks a New Year's resolution.

OVERINDULGENCE

- To strong, hot coffee—
  It's what I'll take
  Tomorrow morning
  For my headache.

- Wine and women, mirth and laughter—
  Sermon and aspirin on the day after.
- "Drink today and drown all sorrow;
  You shall, perhaps, not do it tomorrow."
  —Francis Beaumont & John Fletcher
- To the hangover—something to occupy the head that wasn't used the night before.
- To the irony of intoxication—it makes you feel sophisticated, without being able to pronounce it.
- Here's to the good time I must have had.
- In the words of Dr. Doran,
  "See the wine in the bowl, how it sparkles tonight.
  Tell us what can compete with that red sea of light
  Which breathes forth a perfume that deadens all sorrow,
  And leaves us blessed now, with a headache tomorrow."
- In the words of Lord Byron,
  "Let us have wine and women, mirth and laughter,
  Sermons and soda water the day after.
- Here's to the Ten Stages of Drunkenness:
    1) Witty and charming
    2) Rich and famous
    3) Benevolent
    4) Clairvoyant
    5) Fuck dinner
    6) Patriotic
    7) Crank up the *Enola Gay*
    8) Witty and charming, Part Two
    9) Invisible
       And, finally,
    10) Bulletproof
- What would we like to drink to? To about four in the morning.

- First the man takes a drink;
  Then the drink takes a drink,
  Then the drink takes the man.

- Why is it that my tongue grows loose only when I grow tight?

- To William Temple who summed it up best when he said, "The first glass for myself, the second for my friends; the third for good humor, and the fourth for mine enemies."

- A gilded mirror, a polished bar,
  A million glasses, straws in a jar;
  A courteous young man, all dressed in white,
  Are my recollections of last night!
  And with morning came bags of ice
  So very necessary in this life of vice;
  And when I cooled my throbbing brain,
  Did I swear off and quit? No, I got soused again.

PARENTS

- To my parents who have spoiled me my whole life long—Don't stop!

- To our children, and let us not forget what Joseph Joubert said: they "have more need of models than of critics."

- To the new parents. They will learn, as I did, about babies, that you've got to love them. Unfortunately, you also have to feed them and change them, too. Good luck.

- Here's to my parents—two people who spent half their time wondering how I'd turn out, and the rest of the time when I'd turn in.

- Raise a glass to those who raised us.

- It is written—when children find true love, parents find true joy. Here's to your joy and ours, from this day forward.

PEACE

- May we love peace enough to fight for it.

- May we love peace enough not to fight for it.

- Here's to the proverbial soft answer which turneth away wrath.

- May our leaders be wise, and our commerce increase,
  And may we experience the blessings of peace.

- To peace! In the words of a great general, Dwight David Eisenhower, "We know that there is no true and lasting cure for world tensions in guns and bombs. We know that only the spirit and mind of men, dedicated to justice and right, can, in the long term, enable us to live in the confident tranquility that should be every man's heritage."

- Here's to health, peace, and prosperity—may the flower of love never be nipped by the frost of disappointment, nor the shadow of grief fall among a member of this circle.

POLITICS & POLITICIANS

- To Washington, our country's capital, where the roads, and everything else, go around in circles.

- Here's to the honest politician who, as defined by Simon Cameron, "when he is bought, will stay bought."

- Here's to the politician—a person who straddles an issue when he isn't dodging one.

- To the politician—a person who divides his time between running for office and running for cover.

- Here's to our politician—a man who stands for what he thinks others will fall for.

- To our newly elected officials. May they do only a minimal amount of damage this session.

- To our flag, long may it wave;
  And to our politicians, long may they rave!

- Give us pure candidates and a pure ballot box,
  And our freedom shall stand as firm as the rocks.

PRAISE

- To quote Jonathan Brown, "Whenever the occasion arose, he rose to the occasion."

- Robert Louis Stevenson said, "That man is a success who has lived well, laughed often and loved much; who has gained the respect of intelligent men and the love of children; who has filled his niche and accomplished his task; who leaves the world better than he found it . . . who never lacked appreciation for the earth's beauty or failed to express it; who looked for the best in others and gave the best he had." All this applies to our guest of honor. So here's to him, a true success.

- Lord Barbizon said, "Always behave like a duck—keep calm and unruffled on the surface but paddle like the devil underneath." Here's to someone who follows that philosophy. He's one duck of a fellow.

- Here's to a woman who has so improved her community that she can say, as the great architect Sir Christopher Wren said, "If you seek my monument, look around you."

- To someone who has demonstrated that you can, in fact, teach an old dog new tricks.

- I recognize your remarkable achievements with a line from Shakespeare's *As You Like It:* "You have deserved high commendation, true applause and love."

- If all your marvels one by one,
  I'd toast without much thinking,
  Before the tale was well begun
  I would be dead from drinking.

- To our benefactor, who came forward when we needed him most, proving the old saying, "When it gets dark enough, you will see the stars."

- As Dorothy Parker once said to a friend who had just given birth, "Congratulations: we all knew you had it in you."

PROFESSORS

- To the professor—a woman who talks in her students' sleep.

- To my professor—a textbook wired for sound.

- To our professor—a person whose job it was to tell us how to solve the problems of life which he himself had avoided by becoming a professor.

- To our professor:
  Addition to your friends,
  Subtraction from wants,
  Multiplication of your blessings,
  Division among your foes.

- "Let schoolmasters puzzle their brain
  With grammar and nonsense and learning;
  Good liquor, I stoutly maintain,
  Gives genius a better discerning."
  —Oliver Goldsmith

PROSPERITY

- To a prosperous individual—from what I hear, he doesn't count his money, he measures it.

- May we command success by deserving it.

- May you live as long as you like,
  And have what you like as long as you live.

- When climbing the hill of prosperity, may we never meet a friend coming down.

- Here's to beauty, wit, and wine; and to a full stomach, a full purse, and a light heart.

- In the words of Lord Birkenhead, "Meet success like a gentleman and disaster like a man."

- Here's to success. As Harold Helfer once said, "Success is a bright sun that obscures and makes ridiculously unimportant all the little shadowy flecks of failure."

- To success—making more money to meet obligations you wouldn't have if you didn't make so much money.

- To success—the degree to which other people envy you.

- To prosperity. May each of us always keep the "me" in "economy."

- To prosperity—for, as John Ray said, "Money cures melancholy."

- Here's to health, peace, and prosperity—may the flower of love never be nipped by the frost of disappointment, nor the shadow of grief fall among a member of this circle.

- In the words of Mary L. Booth, "May our feast days be many and our fast days be few."

- Here's to long life and prosperity
  To all of your posterity;
  And those that don't drink with sincerity
  May they be damned to eternity.

- May your shadow never grow less.

- Here's to your promotion. Nothing succeeds like success.

- Here's to caviar when you're hungry,
  Champagne when you're dry,
  All the women you ever want,
  And heaven when you die.

- In the words of *Star Trek*'s Mr. Spock, Live long and prosper."

PSYCHIATRISTS & PSYCHOLOGISTS

- To the psychiatrist, whom Mervyn Stockwood defines as "a man who goes to the Folies-Bergère and looks at the audience."

- To the psychiatrist. He finds you cracked and leaves you broke.

- Let's drink to the psychiatrist—someone whose patients all take their medicine lying down.

- Here's to my shrink, who doesn't understand me.

- To the psychologist. He's even managed to convince himself that he knows what he's talking about.

- Here's to the psychiatrist—a person who doesn't have to worry as long as other people do.

RETIREMENT

- I recognize your remarkable achievements with a line from Shakespeare's *As You Like It:* "You have deserved high commendation, true applause and love."

- I'd love to keep on working, but as Ned Kelly, the Australian outlaw, said as he was being hanged, "Such is life."

- To a man who now has the freedom to do all the things he spent the last forty years dreaming of doing.

- To our former colleague. We don't know what we'll do without him—but we're sure eager to find out.

- To your retirement. A deserved reward for a job well done.

- Here's to the holidays—all 365 of them.

REUNION

- Here's a toast to all who are here,
  No matter where you're from;
  May the best day you have ever seen
  Be worse than the worst to come.

- To the good old days—when we weren't so good, because we weren't so old.

- Your health. May we drink one together in ten years time and a few in between.

- Here's to us that are here, to you that are there, and the rest of us everywhere.

- To friends—as long as we are able
  To lift our glasses from the table.

- "But fill me with the old familiar juice,
  Methinks I might recover bye and bye."
  —Omar Khayyam

- In the immortal words of William Makepeace Thackeray,
  "I drink it as the Fates ordain it,
  Come, fill it, and have done with rhymes;
  Fill up the lonely glass, and drain it
  In memory of dear old times."

- To the good old days—which we are having right now.

- When we are gathered to carouse, my eloquence fails me,
  because there's a silly song that runs through my head,
  "Hail, hail, the gang's all here,
  So what the hell do we care?
  What the hell do we care?
  Hail, hail, the gang's all here,
  So what the hell do we care now?"

SAILING

- Down the hatch!
- May your sails never luff.
- Bottoms up!
- Any port in a storm.

SALESPEOPLE

- Here's to P. T. Barnum who said, "There's a sucker born
  every moment."

- Here's to us. Never sell a salesperson short.

- Here's to opening accounts and closing deals!

119

SEX

- May you live as long as you want to, and want to as long as you live.

- Here's to the game they call Ten Toes;
  It's played all over town.
  The girls all play with ten toes up,
  The boys with ten toes down.

- Here's to you,
  So sweet and good.
  God made you;
  I wish I could.

- Here's to her,
  For whom life holds no terrors.
  Born a virgin, she'll probably die a virgin;
  No hits, no runs, no errors.

- There's been a lot of joshing tonight about sex. But you're not going to goad me into saying anything indiscreet. I'm simply going to fall back on George Bernard Shaw's guarded answer on the topic of sex: "It gives me great pleasure."

- Here's to the girl with the big blue eyes,
  Here's to the girl with the milk-white thighs.
  Our eyes have met, Our thighs, not yet.
  Here's hoping!

SISTERS

- To my sister, whom I forgive. Some part of every family tree has to be out on a limb.

- To my sisters and the secrets we share!

120

- To my sister. We share parents—but not much else.

- We've toasted the mother and the daughter,
  We've toasted the sweetheart and wife;
  But somehow we missed her,
  Our dear little sister—
  The joy of another man's life.

SPEAKERS

- We'll bless our toastmaster,
  Wherever he may roam,
  If he'll only cut the speeches short
  And let us all go home.

- To our speaker. May he rise to the occasion, and sit down soon thereafter.

- To our speaker I give the wisdom of Horace, who said, "Whatever advice you give, be brief."

- Here's to our speaker—may her speech be like a pencil and have a point.

STOCKBROKERS

- Here's to the stockbroker—may your life be full of bulls!

- Here's to the stockbroker—she can tell you what's going to happen next month to your money and explain later why it didn't.

- To the stockbroker—a capitalist who invests himself with other people's money.

TENNIS

- To tennis, the only excuse that some women get for wearing white.

- Here's to tennis—the sport where love means nothing.

- To tennis—may we all have net gains.

- Here's to those who have the guts to be in the tennis racket.

THANKSGIVING

- For what we are about to receive, may the Lord make us truly thankful.

- Here's to the blessing of the year,
  Here's to the friends we hold so dear,
  To peace on earth, both far and near.

- The American eagle and the Thanksgiving turkey—
  May one give us peace in all our states,
  And the other a piece for all our plates.

- Here's to the turkey I'm about to eat and the turkeys I'll eat it with.

TIME

- Best while you have it, use your breath;
  There is no drinking after death.

- "I drink to the days that are!"
  —William Morris

- Don't worry about the future,
  The present is all thou hast,

The future will soon be present,
And the present will soon be past.

- Every day should be passed
  As though it were to be our last.

- May we always look forward with pleasure, and backward without regret.

- In the words of R. A. Campbell, "This is the best day the world has ever seen. Tomorrow will be better."

- Though life now is pleasant
  And sweet to the sense
  We'll be damnably moldy
  A hundred years hence.

- Time cuts down all,
  Both great and small.

- To live in hearts we leave behind is not to die.

TRAVEL

- As Kermit the Frog said, "Wherever you go, there you are."

- "A health to the man on the trail tonight; may his grub hold out; may his dogs keep their legs; may his matches never misfire."
  —Jack London

- "I've traveled many a highway
  I've walked for many a mile
  Here's to the people who made my day
  To the people who waved and smiled."
  —Tom T. Hall

- May the road rise to meet you.
  May the wind be always at your back,

The sun shine warm upon your face,
The rain fall soft upon your fields,
And until we meet again
May God hold you in the hollow of his hand.

- To seasickness—traveling over the water by rail.

- Here's to travel, which, as Benjamin Disraeli said, "teaches toleration."

TRUTH

- May corruption be chained,
  And truth maintained.

- To the power of truth. In the words of Sojourner Truth, "Truth burns up error."

- To truth. As it says in John 8:32, "The truth shall make you free."

- Here's to truth—and no one said it better than Mark Twain when he observed, "If you tell the truth, you don't have to remember anything."

VICTORY

- To the profound ignorance which we brought to this endeavor; because had we known what was ahead, we never would have started.

- Here's to the sweet smell of success.

- Here's to General Douglas MacArthur, who said, "There is no substitute for victory."

124

- To victory. As Alex Haley said, "History is written by the winners."

- Let's have a drink,
  Let's have some fun.
  Because at last
  The job is done.

VISION

- To the man whose vision we are celebrating tonight. He is truly a big man in spirit. As Woodrow Wilson said, "All big men are dreamers."

- Here's to the man with vision—Wayne Gretzky summed it up best when he said, "I skate to where the puck is going to be, not where it has been."

- To the future—may we all work to make it happen.

WEDDING

- Here's a toast to love and laughter and happily ever after.

- Here's to second marriages, which Samuel Johnson described as "the triumph of hope over experience."

- Here's to the new husband
  And here's to the new wife;
  May they remain lovers
  For all of life.

- When children find true love, parents find true joy. Here's to you two, may your joy and ours last forever.

- May you two grow old on one pillow.

- May your wedding days be few and your anniversaries many.

- These two, now standing hand in hand,
  Remind us of our native land.
  For when today they linked their fates,
  They entered the United States.

- Here's to the bride
  And here's to the groom
  And to the bride's father
  Who'll pay for this room.

- To quote Walter Winchell, "Never above you. Never below you. Always beside you."

- Here's to the bride and the groom!
  May you have a happy honeymoon,
  May you lead a happy life,
  May you make a bunch of money soon,
  And live without all strife.

- Down the hatch, to a striking match.

- Here's to the bride and the mother-in-law,
  Here's to the groom and the father-in-law,
  Here's to the sister and brother-in-law,
  Here's to friends and friends-in-law,
  May none of you need an attorney-at-law.

- May you live as long as you want to and may you want to as long as you live.

- To marriage, which Ambrose Bierce defined as "a community consisting of a master, a mistress and two slaves, making in all, two."

- To the happy couple. May all your troubles be little ones.

- As Shakespeare said in *Romeo and Juliet*, may "a flock of blessings light upon thy back."

- "Look down you gods, and on this couple drop a blessed crown."
  —Shakespeare, *The Tempest*

- Here's to my mother-in-law's daughter,
  Here's to her father-in-law's son;
  Here's to the vows we've just taken,
  And the life we've just begun.

- Here's to this fine couple. May their joys be as bright as the morning, and their sorrows but shadows that fade in the sunlight of love.

WINE

- To wine. It improves with age—the older I get, the more I like it.

- God, in his goodness, sent the grapes
  To cheer both great and small;
  Little fools will drink too much,
  And great fools none at all.

- A feast is made for laughter, and wine maketh merry. —Ecclesiastes 10:19

- Drink no longer water, but use a little wine for thy stomach's sake. —1 Timothy 5:23

- Give . . . wine unto those that be of heavy hearts. —Proverbs 31:6

- Wine maketh glad the hearts of man. —Psalms 104:15

- Wine nourishes, refreshes and cheers. Wine is the foremost of medicines . . . wherever wine is lacking, medicines become necessary. —The Talmud

- Wine, which cheereth gods and men. —Judges 9:13

- I'm partial to the logic of James Howell who once said,
  "Good wine makes good blood;
  Good blood causeth good humors;
  Good humors cause good thoughts;
  Good thoughts bring forth good works;
  Good works carry a man to heaven.
  Ergo: Good wine carrieth a man to heaven."

- To quote George Sterling,
  "He who clinks his cup with mine,
  Adds a glory to the wine."

- Wine and women—may we always have a taste for both.

- To women and wine—both are sweet poison.

- "'Tis a pity," said Lord Byron,
  "Wine should be so deleterious,
  For tea and coffee leave us much more serious."

- Here's to wine, wit, and wisdom:
  Wine enough to sharpen wit,
  Wit enough to give zest to wine,
  Wisdom enough to "shut down" at the right time.

- The best wine . . . goeth down sweetly, causing the lips of
  those that are asleep to speak. —Song of Solomon 7:9

- Wine was created from the beginning to make men joyful,
  and not to make men drunk. Wine drunk with moderation is
  the joy of the soul and the heart. —Ecclesiasticus 31:27–28

- In the words of Jonathan Swift, "This wine should be eaten,
  it is too good to be drunk."

- To wine—those plump grapes' immortal juice
  That does this happiness produce.

- "This bottle's the sun of our table.
  Its beams are rosy wine;

We, planets that are not able
Without its help to shine."
—Richard Brinsley Sheridan

- To wine—may those who use it never abuse it.

- "Then fill the cup, fill high! fill high!
Nor spare the rosy wine,
If death be in the cup, we'll die—
Such death would be divine."
—James Russell Lowell

- Here's to the red and sparkling wine,
I'll be your sweetheart, if you'll be mine,
I'll be constant, I'll be true,
I'll leave my happy home for you.

- Fill up boys, and drink a bout;
Wine will banish sorrow!
Come, drain the goblet out;
We'll have more tomorrow!

- Wine, to strengthen friendship and light the flame of love.

- "Give me a bowl of wine—in this I bury all unkindness."
—Shakespeare, *Julius Caesar*

- Drink to me only with thine eyes,
And I will pledge with mine;
For I would have to pawn my watch
If you should drink more wine.

- To grape expectations.

- "God made man,
Frail as a bubble.
God made love,
Love made trouble.
God made the vine,
Was it a sin

That man made wine
To drown trouble in?"
—Oliver Herford

- Here's to the man
Who owns the land
That bears the grapes
That make the wine
That tastes as good
As this does.

- Here's to mine and here's to thine!
Now's the time to clink it!
Here's a bottle of fine old wine,
And we're all here to drink it.

- Here's to old wine and young women.

WISDOM

- May we live to learn well, and learn to live well.

- In the words of Charles M. Meyers, "May you have the hindsight to know where you've been, the foresight to know where you're going, and the insight to know you've gone too far."

- Here's to wine, wit, and wisdom.
Wine enough to sharpen wit,
Wit enough to give zest to wine,
Wisdom enough to "shut down" at the right time.

- To wisdom—may we always learn from our mistakes.

- "Ask nothing that is not clearly right, and submit to nothing that is wrong."
—Andrew Jackson

- Here's to wisdom. May it come with age.

WOMEN

- Here's to woman, whose heart and whose soul
  Are the light and the life of each path we pursue;
  Whether sunned at the tropics or chilled at the pole,
  If woman be there, there's happiness too.

- Here's to old wine and young women.

- Here's to woman, who in our hours of ease
  Is uncertain, coy, and impossible to please.

- Here's to the beautiful woman—the hell of the soul, the purgatory of the wallet, and the paradise of the eyes.

- To woman—a paradox who puzzles when she pleases and pleases when she puzzles.

- To quote Minna Thomas Antrim, Here's to women, who are "clever enough to convince us that we are cleverer than they at their cleverest."

- To a woman's tongue: only three inches long, but it can kill a man six feet tall.

- Here's to woman, the source of all our bliss;
  There's a special taste of heaven in her kiss;
  But from the queen upon her throne, to the maid in the dairy,
  They are all alike in one respect—
  They are all quite contrary.

- Here's to women—they're the loveliest flowers that bloom under heaven.

- "I have a dozen healths to drink to these fair ladies."
  —Shakespeare, *Henry VIII*

- Here's to women, the sweethearts, the wives,
  The delights of our firesides by night and by day,

Who never do anything wrong in their lives,
Except when permitted to have their own way.

- Let her be clumsy, or let her be slim,
  Young or ancient, I care not a feather;
  So fill up a goblet, fill it to the brim,
  Let us toast all the ladies together.

- "Drink to fair woman, who, I think,
  Is most entitled to it:
  For if anything ever can drive me to drink,
  She certainly could do it."
  —B. Jabez Jenkins

- To women—the crown of creation.

- To women and wine—both are sweet poison.

- To wine and women—may we always have a taste for both.

- Here's to women, the ultimate aristocrats—they elect without voting, govern without law, and decide without appeal.

- Women—the fairest work of creation; the edition being extensive, let no man be without a copy.

- Here's to the ladies—first in our hearts and first in our wallets.

- Here's to woman—the fair magician who can turn man into an ass and make him think he's a lion.

- May we kiss all the women we please, and please all the women we kiss.

- Here's to our sweethearts and our wives;
  May our sweethearts soon become our wives,
  And our wives ever remain our sweethearts.

- Here's to the gladness when she's glad,
  Here's to the sadness of her sadness when she's sad;
  But the gladness of her gladness,

And the sadness of her sadness,
Are nothing compared to the madness of her madness when
she's mad.

- A toast of wine, to woman divine,
I would drink in haste, me think;
To her eyes, to her hair, to her beauty so rare—
But I haven't the wine to drink.

- Here's to the ladies—you can't live with them and you can't
live without them.

- Here's to woman—a mistress of arts, who robs a man of his
bachelor's degree and forces him by lectures to study philosophy.

- The ladies, God bless them,
May nothing distress them.

- Here's to the prettiest, here's to the wittiest,
Here's to the truest of all who are true,
Here's to the nearest one, here's to the sweetest one,
Here's to them, all in one—here's to you.

- Here's to the woman—my sweetheart and my wife,
She's never done anything wrong in her life.
It took me some time for my soul I did fear,
But finally I learned this lesson most dear.

- Here's to the woman that's good and sweet,
Here's to the woman that's true,
Here's to the woman that rules my heart—
In other words, here's to you.

- To the ladies—we admire them for their beauty, respect
them for their intelligence, adore them for their virtues, and
love them because we can't help it.

- In the immortal words of Ambrose Bierce, "Here's to woman—ah, that we could fall into her arms without falling into her hands."

- To woman—the only loved autocrat who governs without law; and decides without appeal.

- Here's to the light that lies in women's eyes,
  And lies, and lies, and lies.

- May our women distrust men in general, but not us in particular.

- Here's to God's first thought, Man!
  Here's to God's second thought, Woman!
  Second thoughts are always best,
  So here's to Woman!

- "What, sir, would the people of earth be without woman? They would be scarce, sir, almighty scarce."
  —Mark Twain

- To the lovely ladies. May they always heed the wise words of Ralph Waldo Emerson, who said, "The only gift is a portion of thyself."

- "And nature swears, the lovely dears
  Her noblest work she classes, O;
  Her 'prentice hand she tried on man,
  And then she made the lasses, O."
  —Robert Burns

- To women, whose beauty and wisdom are proof of the existence of a higher power.

- Here's to the girl with the big blue eyes,
  Here's to the girl with the milk-white thighs.
  Our eyes have met; our thighs, not yet.
  Here's hoping!

- Here's to the girls of the American shore,
  I love but one, I love no more;
  Since she's not here to drink her part,
  I drink her share with all my heart.

- To a grand old lady who has gotten better with age, I recite
  the famous lyrics "The old gray mare ain't what she used
  to be."

- Here's to the girl with eyes of blue,
  Whose heart is kind and love is true;
  Here's to the girl with eyes of brown,
  Whose spirit proud you cannot down;
  Here's to the girl with eyes of gray,
  Whose sunny smile drives care away:
  Whate'er the hue of their eyes may be,
  I drink to the girls, this toast with thee!

- Here's to a girl who's bound to win
  Her share at least of blisses,
  Who knows enough not to go in
  When it is raining kisses.

- Here's to lasses we've loved, my lad,
  Here's to the lips we've pressed;
  For of kisses and lasses,
  Like liquor and glasses,
  The last is always the best.

WORK

- May we always follow the wise advice of Henry David Thoreau to "Do what you love"—and may we always love what
  we do.

- To the truth behind Freud's definition of normality as the ability to love—and to work.

- To work—the easiest device man has invented to escape boredom.

- "May the work that you have
  Be the play that you love."
  —E. Geberding

- Here's to work—may we never be without it.

Do you have a special toast you've collected or made up? If so, send it to:

Crisp Toasts
c/o St. Martin's Press
175 Fifth Avenue
New York, NY 10010

We're sorry that no compensation or credit can be given, but if it's appropriate, we'll include it in the next edition of *Crisp Toasts*.

W.R.E. III & A.F.